'By any standards these are indeed remarkable islands.
It is difficult to imagine anyone – island fanatic or not, birdwatcher or not – failing
to enjoy such a fascinating story.'
BRITISH BIRDS

Although they are now deserted by man, the Saltee Islands have an
exciting and controversial past. They are one of the
world's major bird sanctuaries. This book details the islands'
history from the Stone Age, through early Christian times, the
Vikings
and Normans, and the days when the islands were a bustling haven
for pirates and smugglers. It also looks in depth at the islands'
200 species of birds – some of them rare – their breeding
habits, migratory movements and general ecology.

SALTEES

First published 1977 by
The O'Brien Press Ltd.
20 Victoria Road
Dublin 6.
First paperback edition 1987
ISBN 0-86278-147-7

10 9 8 7 6 5 4 3 2

Cover Pictures Richard Mills
Book design and cover Michael O'Brien
Typesetting Redsetter Ltd. and
Phototype-Set Ltd.
Printed by
Richard Clay Ltd.

Authors: Richard Roche (left in picture)
was born and reared near the coast of
South Wexford. For many years he was
Deputy and Literary Editor of the Irish
Independent. As a youth he spent many
summers as a trawler-hand on Kilmore
Quay boats fishing around the Saltees. He
is best-known as an historian and his
books include *Here's Their Memory* and
The Norman Invasion of Ireland.
Oscar Merne (right in picture) works for
the research branch of the Forest &
Wildlife Service. For 10 years he was
Warden of the Wexford Wildfowl
Reserve. Known internationally, he is the
author of numerous books and scientific
papers.

*Previous page – A view of the Gannet
colony from the seaward side. The birds can
be seen nesting very close to the summit of
the cliff.
If undisturbed by human visitors the colony
might well extend over the top onto the flat
ground. Note the immature bird in flight on
the right, showing its dark tail and black-
flecked wings.*

SALTEES

Islands of birds and legends

RICHARD ROCHE

with a section on the bird life by
OSCAR MERNE

photographs by

George Gmelch
Brendan Hearne
Richard Mills

THE O'BRIEN PRESS
DUBLIN

Contents

Preface

For pirate-infested waters, islands with smuggling traditions and tales of cutlass-swinging sea rovers, one does not have to sail as far as the West Indies or the Cocos Islands.

In the waters of Ireland, off the south coast of Wexford, lie two islands which have a long and romantic association with pirates, loot-filled caves and signal lights winking in the darkness. These are the Saltee Islands, lying a few miles south of Kilmore Quay, now uninhabited but once the haunt of privateers and smugglers. Nor does the Saltees' history begin and end with these colourful characters. In the dim dawn of the story of man in Ireland the islands were among the first places inhabited by primitive New Stone Age settlers.

Here, too, dwelt early Christian hermits, leaving traces of their habitation to tantalise the archaeologist. In medieval times there were probably other monks, perhaps members of the Tintern Abbey community to which the Saltees had been granted.

But the era of the pirate and the smuggler, in the 17th and 18th centuries, thrust the islands into the international limelight. The ships of England, Ireland, France and America, to mention but a few, fought for supremacy of the waters around the islands. Into them also ventured the marauding corsairs of the Barbary Coast, the Algerines, the Biskeyners, Dunkirkers and Yankees, seeking booty and hostages, stealing cattle from the islanders, using the Saltee caves as storehouses for their loot and provisions.

It is not difficult to conjure up pictures of those brigands as one walks along the cliffs of the Great Saltee today: there below, in that huge cavern, dimly-lighted by flickering torches, sit the pirate captains. Bales, casks, and boxes are piled high above the full tide mark. The pirates, bearded, dark-skinned men, drink the best of Government supplied rum, finger fine silks, dispute the value of some hides, divide captured food supplies, maybe occasionally fight among themselves. If you listen with your inner ear you may hear their shouts and laughter over the raucous cries of thousands of sea birds.

The 18th century was the century of the smuggler, most of whom would have preferred to call themselves importers and exporters baulked by discriminatory navigation laws and other decrees levelled against Irish trade and traders by a greedy neighbour state. Towards the end of the century the wars between Britain and France prevented legitimate trade between Ireland and the Continent, — and 18th century gentlemen, in Wexford and elsewhere, liked their glass of wine and goblet of brandy. Many contraband cargoes were transhipped behind the Saltees and taken ashore in smaller boats to the Lough of Lingstown. But the day of the smuggler soon ended. When the Napoleonic Wars finished with the Battle of Waterloo in 1815, the British Navy turned its attention to the smugglers and wiped them out within ten years.

The Saltees were to jump just once more into the international headlines about this time. In a cave on the bigger island, two of the leaders of the 1798 insurrection in Wexford, Beauchamp Bagenal Harvey and John Henry Colclough, were captured. Taken to Wexford, they were summarily tried and executed in a manner that was to cause much embarrassment to the British Government later. After that, the Saltees returned to more peaceful ways of life, — being profitably farmed throughout the 19th century, then becoming the favourite rabbit-hunting locale for several generations of sportsmen.

Their scenic beauty and amazing numbers and variety of wild birds drew constantly increasing boat-loads of visitors, most of whom arrived and left without being aware of the long and exciting history of the islands them-selves. It is in an effort to fill that gap in visitors' knowledge that this book on the history, topography, legends and birdlife of the Saltees has been compiled. Some of the information supplied may be new even to those who live and work within sight of the Saltees. Much of the lore of the islands will be familiar to local people, but will, it is hoped, be fascinating to others.

The compilation of all of it has been a labour of love for the authors, both of whom trust that this book will be accepted as a tribute to the sturdy, industrious, kindly people of south Wexford, whose history is intertwined in the stirring saga of the Saltees.

This map of South Wexford includes many of the places mentioned in this book.

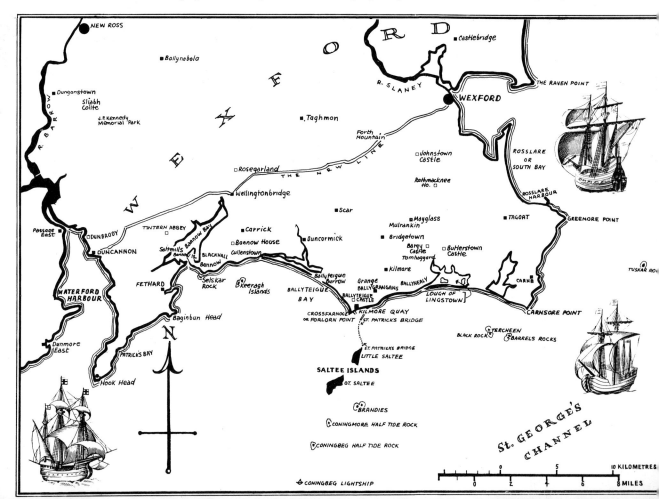

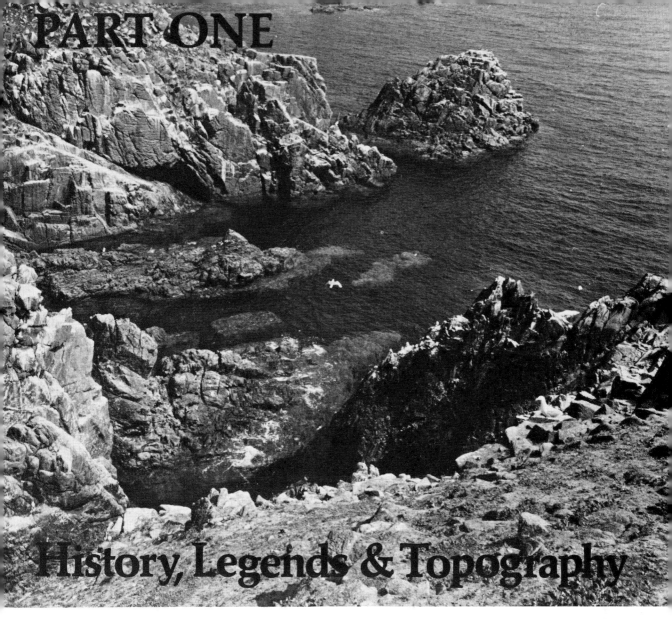

PART ONE

History, Legends & Topography

A general view of the deeply indented cliffscape at the centre of the southern side of Great Saltee.

Vital statistics of the Saltees

Location — Latitude 52 degrees 8' 30'' North; Longitude 6 degrees 41' West.
Off south coast of Wexford.

Distance from shore — Great Saltee, 3¼ statute miles; Little Saltee, 2½ statute
miles, from Kilmore Quay.

Area — Great Saltee, 219 statute acres, 1 rood and 29 perches;
Little Saltee, 92 acres, 2 roods and 5 perches.

Highest point — South Summit, Great Saltee, 198 feet.

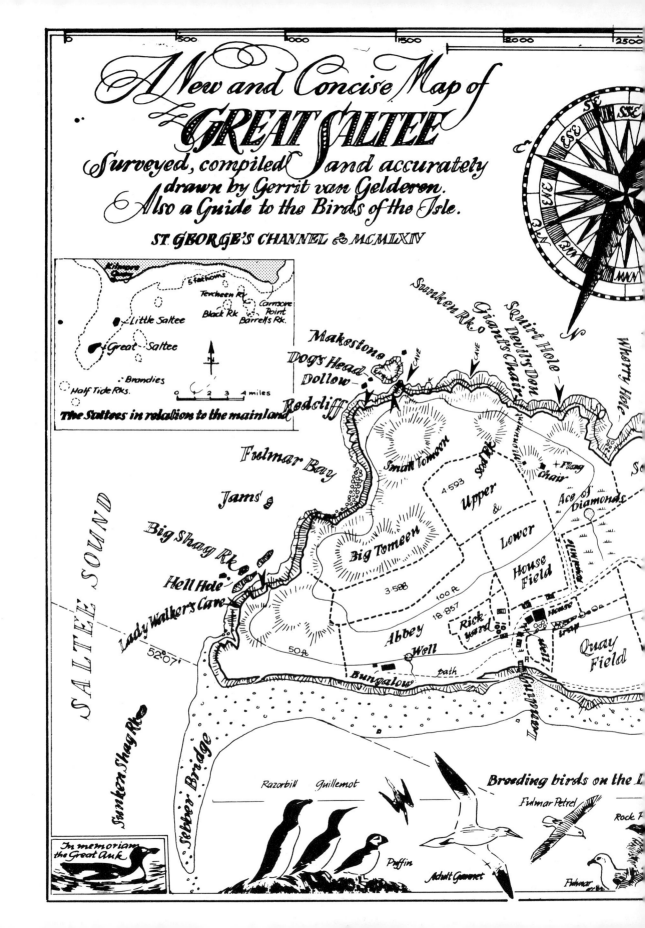

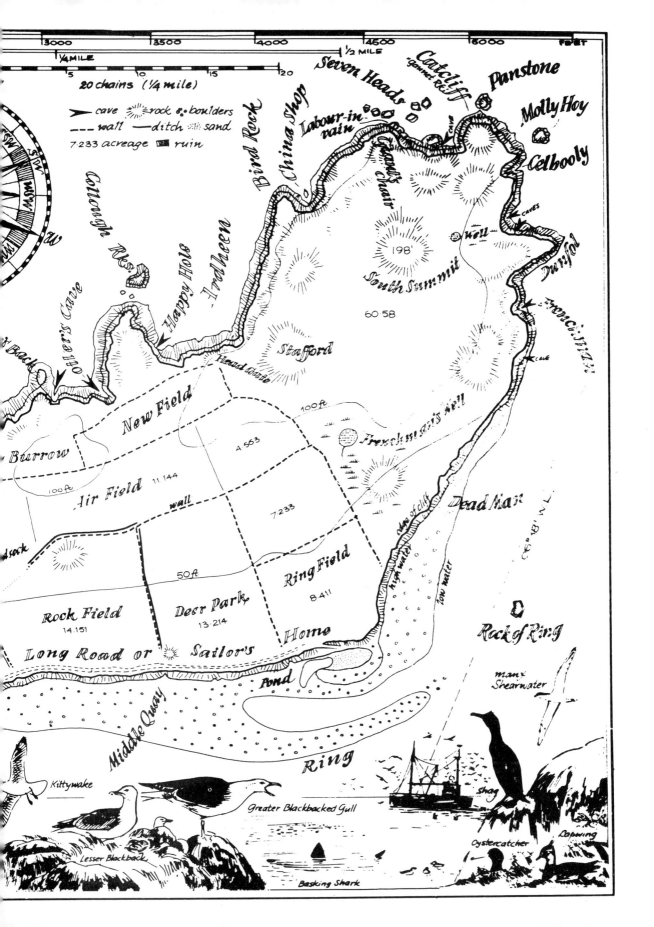

Map Labels

Scale: 3000 · 3500 · 4000 · 4500 · 5000 FEET
¼ MILE · ½ MILE
20 chains (¼ mile)
5 · 10 · 15 · 20

Legend:
➤ cave · ✺ rock · ⦂ boulders
--- wall · — ditch · ▒ sand
7.233 acreage · ▩ ruin

Catcliff (sunnet reef)
Panstone
Seven Heads
Molly Hoy
Labour-in-vain
Celbooly
China Shop
Bird Rock
Giant's Chair
CAVE
Cotlough Rks
CAVES
Well
Ardheen
Happy Hole
Dunjor
198'
South Summit
60·58
Otter's Cave
Frenchman's Well
Stafford
Head Gate
100 ft
New Field
Burrow
4·563
Frenchman's Well
Air Field
11·144
100 ft
Dead Man
wall
7·233
Edge of cliff
High water
Low water
50 ft
Ring Field
8·411
Rock Field
14·151
Deer Park
13·214
Home
Rock of Ring
Long Road or Sailor's
Pond
Manx Shearwater
Middle Quay
Ring
Shag
Kittywake
Greater Blackbacked Gull
Lesser Blackback
Oystercatcher
Lapwing
Basking Shark

Chapter 1
Distant Views

The first distant views of the Saltee Islands from the south Wexford mainland are got from Forth Mountain, in the east, and Sliabh Coilte,[1] in the west of the county. From the New Line,[2] the military road linking Wexford town with Duncannon Fort, built by the British after the insurrection of 1798, the first glimpse of the islands is caught as the road curves in a south-westerly direction around the shoulder of Forth Mountain — The Mountain to all who live in south Wexford, even though it rises to little more than 700 feet above sea level.

The islands, from the mountain road, seem to lie deceptively near the coast, fern-green on the blue sea of summer, lichen-grey against the darker waters of winter.

From a viewing-point on the southern flank of Sliabh Coilte, overlooking the verdant neatness of the John F. Kennedy Memorial Aboretum,[3] they seem even closer to the coast — a mere handspan from the church and village of Kilmore Quay.

As one travels deeper into the Barony of Bargy, in the east, or Shelburne, in the west, other less distant views of the islands come into focus. From the Rock of Scar or the Hill of Carrig they begin to show some of their topographical features, such as fields, cliffs and ruins.

From the sea-girt vantage point of Baginbun,[4] to the west, a new perspective opens up the gap between isles and mainland and places them in their true location two and a half and three and a quarter miles out in St. George's Channel. But the most dramatic view of all has to be awaited until one passes through the neat fishing village of Kilmore Quay, its one long, meandering street leading southwards between trim, thatched, white-washed cottages until it reaches a crest at the Star of the Sea church. Here, with a suddenness that is startling, a vast sea-vista opens up — the rocky coastline of south Wexford running away to the east where lie Carnsore Point (the Hieron. Akron, or Holy Promontory, of Ptolemy[5]) and Tuskar Rock;[6] the sandhills and curving strand of the Burrow[7] sweeping away on the other hand to the west where the fingers of Baginbun and Hook Head[8] jut into the ocean; and in the centre, above and beyond the harbour wall, the Saltee Islands themselves.

Top — The harbour at Kilmore Quay today, with the Saltees dim on the horizon. At low tide the broken break-water (centre, foreground) and end of the old quay wall (right foreground) can be seen.

Above — White-washed, thatched cottages line the long street of Kilmore Quay, Co. Wexford's most picturesque village.

From here, before one descends to the quay, the islands can be best seen. The Little Saltee, nearest the mainland, lying like a seal in the water; the Great Saltee, further out, raising its bulk higher out of the tidal reaches of the Channel.

Their outlines are smooth, rounded as they have been by pre-historic ice, by wind and by water.[9] The higher ground at each end of the Great Saltee seems, at a distance, to be the only remarkable topographical feature. There are no big trees, so the old boundaries of farms and fields are easily traced.

You might be forgiven for dismissing the Saltees as desolate, uninhabited and uninteresting islands, hardly worth a visit. How wrong you would be!

Geographically and geologically the islands are unique among the isles off the coast of Ireland. From Ireland's Eye, off Co. Dublin, to Sherkin, off the extreme south-west tip of Co. Cork, the Saltees are the only islands along this vast stretch of Irish coast.

Geologically they are among the oldest pieces of land in either Ireland or Britain, formed as they are of Pre-Cambrian granitoid gneiss.[10]

They have, down the centuries, been the home of early Celts, the site of a Patrician-era monastic settlement, the focus of Norse sea-raiders (who may have given them their name), the haunt of pirates and smugglers, the refuge of political leaders on the run, the peaceful habitat of farmers and fishermen, and the nesting-place of hundreds of thousands of exotic sea-birds.

Today the islands are uninhabited — except by the birds, rabbits and rats. But the Saltees still loom large in the lives of the people of south Wexford. Their landmarks are essential to the inshore fishermen who trawl and set their lobster-pots in the waters around the islands — Kilmore Quay lobsters are relished in London, Paris and other European cities. The islands are indispensable to local weather-forecasters — when they seem distant, for instance, the weather will be fine; when they appear near, there is usually rain on the way, and, as the wits say, when you cannot see the Saltees at all, then the rain has already arrived.

Occasionally the islands jump into the news headlines — with a bird-watching party marooned by bad weather, a cliff fatality or a shipwreck. These are the occasions when the local people prefer not to see the Saltees in the news. Rather would they wish the islands to stay as they normally are — the peaceful habitat of wild birds and animals, a beautiful place for picnic and boating trips, a familiar yet slightly mysterious feature of the south Wexford seascape. Mariners and fishermen have learned to respect the islands and their treacherous surrounding tidal waters — in an area known as "the graveyard of a thousand ships" the Saltees must be two of its most sinister tombstones.

Some of their mystery springs from the fact that, fertile though they are, and mild their climate, the Saltees were among the first of the islands off the Irish coast to be deserted by their inhabitants. Before the Blaskets, or Innishmurray (off Co. Sligo), or Owey (off Co. Donegal) were abandoned the Saltees were left to the wild birds and the rabbits.

Perhaps it is this salient feature — the absence of people where people once lived and should live — that adds a sombre mystery to these islands. They seem to be haunted by the ghosts of the past — a past that is rich in history and legend.

Yet they are, in many ways, a comforting sight, not merely to the returning trawlers and lobster-boats chugging back to Kilmore Quay from the nearby fishing-grounds, but also to the country folk living inland — an immutable, unchanging presence and a symbol of the historic past. They may not know much about the Saltees but to the people of south Wexford they are *the islands,* as if no other islands existed anywhere else round the coast of Ireland.

As we review their topography, history and legends we may be tempted to agree with that view.

FOOTNOTES

1.   One of the insurgent camps was situated on Sliabh Coilte in 1798 and it was from here that the only "naval" action of the insurrection was launched in June, 1798, when a British gunboat was captured on the Barrow.

2.   The New Line is the local name for the military road built after 1798. When the loyalist garrison withdrew from Wexford town to Duncannon Fort on May 30 in that year they retreated through the southern baronies of Forth, Bargy and Shelburne, burning and pillaging as they went. The resultant hatred among the people precluded any further retreats by the military by the same route. (See *The Wexford Rising* by Charles Dickson, pp.87-88).

3.   The Kennedy Memorial Park (410 acres) was opened in May, 1968, and dedicated to the memory of John Fitzgerald Kennedy, President of the U.S.A. from 1961 to 1963. The Park overlooks the Kennedy ancestral home at Dunganstown, a mile away.

4.   Baginbun is noted as the place where Raymond "Le Gros" Fitzgerald landed in May, 1170, with a small party of Normans, Flemings and Welsh, in the fourth incursion of the Norman invasion. The name Baginbun is probably a corruption of Bec a Banne, Old French for "the promontory at or near Banne (Bannow)".

5.   Ptolemy, second-century Greek geographer. P. W. Joyce (*The origin and history of Irish names of places,* 1875) says Ptolemy's work "is only a corrected copy of another written by Marinus of Tyre, who lived a short time before him, and the latter is believed to have drawn his materials from an ancient Tyrian atlas". Ptolemy does not note the Saltees, however.

6.   Tuskar Rock, a dangerous granite rock seven miles off-shore which, before a lighthouse was built there in 1815, was a death-trap for ships bound for Liverpool after crossing the Atlantic.

7.   The Burrow comprises about six miles of sand-hills fronted by a curving, steeply-shelved beach between Crossfarnogue and Bar O' Lough and it forms a promontory separating the former tidal lagoons of Ballyteigue and Broadwater from the sea. With the building of a sea-wall and sluice gates at The Cull, these lagoons were reclaimed as a relief scheme during the Famine years. The Burrow itself consists of Aeolian drift, dating from pre-historic times. Its flora is extensive and distinctive. The sea-inlet behind the Burrow with its dangerous opening at Bar O' Lough, was once known as Mablenhaven and carried much coaster-trade in former times.

8.   "The Saltee Islands stand fearlessly amid the dashing waves — and the far-off Tower of Hook terminates the sea view"   Mrs. S. C. Hall in *Sketches of Irish Character* (1845). The Tower of Hook is the lighthouse on Hook Head and is believed to be the oldest lighthouse in Europe. Christian monks kept a warning fire burning there from the 5th century. Later a crude, raised structure of stone, earth and timber held a beacon fire in an iron basket. The present tower, added to and modernised, is more than 750 years old.

9.   For much of the geological data in this and other sections of the book, I am indebted to Dr. Edward Culleton, of An Foras Taluntais, and to Dr. Michael D. Max, of the Irish Geological Survey.

10. See *Memoirs of the Geological Survey — Explanatory Memoir of the Geological Survey of Ireland,* by G. H. Kinahan, 1879.

Top — Kilmore Quay in the 1930s, with two fishermen baiting lobster pots and a typical trawler of the times moored behind. A still from the Rosslare Strand Hotel film on the Saltees.

Right — Jack Devereux sculls a dingy from his fishing-boat to the landing place amid the rocks on the northern shore of the Great Saltee.

Chapter 2
As old as the Saltees!

The saying "as old as the hills" could, with more accuracy, be altered to "as old as the Saltees", for these islands are formed of rock which is among the oldest in Western Europe.[1] Because of this they are geologically unique in Ireland and of immense interest to geologists.

The Pre-Cambrian bedrock[2] of the islands may be anything from 600 million to 2,000 million years old. It is composed largely of granite or granitoid gneiss, with minor basic dykes. These rocks are extremely hard and erode very slowly — even when opposed to the fearsome force of the seas that lash the Saltees. But thousands of years of storms and ravenous waves have eaten into the rocks of the islands and left jagged cliffs and crags, deep caves and weird rock formations round their shores, especially on the exposed westerly, southerly and easterly sections. Islanders and Kilmore Quay fishermen have given many descriptive names to these island places — Cat Cliff, Labour-In-Vain (a bridge-like rock formation), China-shop, Happy Hole (a high-roofed cave), Devil's Den, Giant's Chair, Hell Hole, Tommeen, Ardheen, Makeston[3] and many others.

The islands owe more of their features to glacial action. These include the rounded shapes and numerous "raised beaches" and also much of the drift that is the clay, sand and gravel with which the bedrock is covered.

The "raised beaches" — and there are many along the south Wexford coast from Kilmore to Bannow — are the subject of considerable controversy among geologists who disagree about their age. Basically they are the remnants of beaches deposited when the sea-level was about four metres higher than it now is. They consist of rounded pebbles often compacted by fine sand and the weight of other overlying material.

Some geologists assign these "raised beaches" to a high sea-level during the last interglacial period; others assign them to the penultimate or, as it is some-times called, the Great Interglacial period. As the climate became colder with the onset of each glacial epoch, rocks were shattered and comminuted to fine gravel and sand by successive freeze-thaw processes. This shattered material, known as "head", is usually found overlying the "raised beaches".

During the last glaciation, termed the "Midlandian" and dated between 20,000 and 10,000 B.C., an ice sheet advanced from the Irish Sea, depositing calcareous marine till along the east and south-east coasts of Co. Wexford. This marine till or glacial drift, containing as it does calcium carbonate, is particularly fertile. The Saltee Islands were enveloped by this ice mass which, on thawing, deposited a covering of loam to clay-loam texture. Where the solid rock protrudes the till has moved down-slope on to the flatter ground.

But this ice sheet left more dramatic evidence of its pre-historic presence in the area. Great boulders of the pinkish, coarse-grained granite which are found at Carnsore Point were left scattered on the beaches of the islands and of the mainland. At Neamestown,[4] not far from Kilmore Quay, several such glacial erratics can be seen, the most remarkable being the huge boulder called St. Patrick's Rock or St. Patrick's Boat.

One geologist has also stated that the curious ridge of rocks and shingle, called St. Patrick's Bridge, curving out from the mainland at Neamestown and running, partly submerged and partly tidal now, to the Little Saltee, is an eroded glacial moraine. His theory is that this ridge marked the limit of the Irish Sea ice sheet which, when it melted, deposited its load of boulders, stones and shingle in a great ridge between the mainland and the Saltees.

There is another view, however, about the origin of this curious topographical feature. Writing in 1879, G. H. Kinahan, M.R.I.A.,[5] commented: "These islands (The Saltees) lie to the south of the mainland and are connected

Waves pound themselves into white foam at the foot of the high cliffs on the southern shore of the Great Saltee.

The long, shingly bar of St. Patrick's Bridge curves out from the mainland at Neamestown towards the Saltees (background). The big rock on the left is known as St. Patrick's Rock.

with it by a bar or ridge that is partially submerged and partly tidal, the latter portion being called St. Patrick's Bridge. These bars between the mainland and the little Saltee, and between the two islands, are evidently due to the colliding of the tidal currents on the west and east of the islands. On the east of St. Patrick's Bridge are some large blocks, the residue of the drift that has been cut away by the sea, the largest being called St. Patrick's Boat, from a legend connected with it. It is a remarkably large erratic".

The legend to which Kinahan alludes relates how St. Patrick, wishing to visit the Saltees, borrowed a boat from a local fisherman. The vessel, however, leaked and sank within a few score yards of the beach, and the saint had to swim ashore. Wet and angry, he cursed the boat which immediately turned to stone. Patrick then started to build a ridge of rocks out to the Little Saltee, which he eventually reached dry-footed!

Another, even more colourful, tale describes a cross-country chase of the Devil by St. Patrick which started in the Galtee Mountains and ended at the Saltees, more than 100 miles away. Hotly pursued by the saint, the Devil bit a huge lump out of the Devil's Bit mountain to get through the hills, leaving a gap called, to this day, the Devil's Bit. With this in his mouth he raced on south-eastwards into Co. Kilkenny and then into Co. Wexford. Racing over Forth Mountain, St. Patrick grabbed a huge boulder to fling at the retreating Devil who, by this time, was nearing Kilmore. At Neamestown Old Nick took to the sea and started swimming out, the "Bit" still in his mouth.

St. Patrick flung the huge boulder after him and it landed about 500 yards out — today it is called St. Patrick's Rock and the saint's finger marks are said to be visible on its top. Frustrated, Patrick then collected rocks on the shore and pelted the swimming demon with them. In this way St. Patrick's

Bridge was formed. The Devil continued swimming on his way but, two-and-a-half miles from shore, a portion of the "Bit" fell from his mouth — and formed the Little Saltee. Half a mile further on, the remaining portion of the "Bit", a bigger chunk, fell out — and we got the Great Saltee.

And that, dear reader, is why the old people say the Saltees belong to Tipperary![6]

More curious still is the following note found in an unpublished manuscript belonging to the late Kathleen Browne, historian, of Rathronan Castle, Bridgetown, Co. Wexford:

"In the last century the Saltees were owned by a Tipperary gentleman. He was in Wexford and being in need of money borrowed it from Grogan of Johnstown (Castle) saying: 'If I do not return, to pay you, you may have the Saltees'. He was killed shortly afterwards and Grogan claimed the islands. Mr. Furlong, father of the Furlongs of the Wooden House, was the tenant of the islands. Acting under legal advice he refused to pay the rent to Grogan for some time, till he (Grogan) offered him a lease at a very low rent. He took the lease, paid the rent and Grogan became the undisputed owner. The moment the lease was out Furlong was evicted... T. Fitzgibbon told me that he heard it many times stated in Tipperary that the Saltees formed part of the Liberties of Cashel and were at one time the property of the Corporation of that city'.

Griffiths, in his *Chronicles of the County Wexford,*[7] quotes a further legend which holds that the saint commenced building the "bridge" with the view of continuing it to France! St. Patrick did, apparently, visit these parts on his missionary journeys throughout Ireland. The "Tripartite Life" of the saint states that he visited "Hy-Kinsellagh as far as the southern extremity of the Province".

Dr. Gabriel O'C. Redmond, in his *History and Topography of the Parish of Hook* adds further to this: "The southern extremity of the Province to which the great Apostle penetrated was the Peninsula of Hook, where St. Dubhan flourished about the same time, and in all probability he visited the Pilgrim of the Hook on this occasion. On the eastern coast of the Peninsula there is a bay called Patrick's Bay, about half a mile south of Brecan's Church, where, perhaps, St. Patrick landed. On the north coast of the Lesser Saltee Island is marked, on the Ordnance Survey map, St. Patrick's Bridge. The Great Apostle may have sailed round the coast of Wexford, visiting the various Christian missionaries and pilgrims who had established primitive mariners' churches along the coast from Carnsore to the Hook".

Whether Patrick ever visited the Kilmore area, or the Saltees, cannot now be confirmed; and whatever wondrous works he performed elsewhere in Ireland, he certainly did not build the "bridge" between Neamestown and the Little Saltee that bears his name to this day. Later generations, however, probably blessed his legendary feat while making use of St. Patrick's Bridge as a causeway to get to the smaller island. This rather hazardous way of getting to the Little Saltee is mentioned in ancient documents where the "Bridge" is called "a common causeway", and as late as the 1840s farmers drove cattle across on the "causeway" to graze on the island.

Whatever the origin of the "Bridge" — either glacial moraine or tidal bar — there has always been a healthy respect among local boatmen for its hidden rocks and treacherous currents. "The tide boils over it like water in a boiling pot," one old fisherman has said. Until fairly recently, Kilmore Quay boats tried to avoid passing over the submerged "Bridge" on their way back to port — often detouring through the Sound (between the two Saltees) rather than risking the turbulent passage across the "Bridge". [8]

Robert Lloyd Praeger, who visited the Saltees in the early years of the present century, describes the Great Saltee thus:[9]

"It rises from a boulder-beach on the north side, over a rough grassy surface overlying boulder-clay, to a height of about 200 feet, where it breaks down in a rocky scarp to a sea which is often turbulent, for the island lies fully open to south-west gales sweeping in from the Atlantic... The area of tillage can still be traced, but it is now fully occupied by native plants, including great quantities of luxuriant Wild Hyacinths, while the seaward parts are gardens of Sea-pink, Sea Campion and Scurvy Grass."

Under good management the soils of the Saltees are capable of producing high-quality pastures. They are also generally suited to a wide range of agricultural and horticultural crops, and are well-adapted to tillage crops such as wheat, barley, oats, potatoes and sugar-beet. Special crops such as early potatoes, onions, carrots and beans can be grown in these soils, favoured by an extremely mild climate with little or no frost. Crops, and indeed all vegetation, face one local hazard — salt spray from the gigantic waves that crash at storm-times against the Saltee cliffs and crags. This spray flies right over the islands, drenching everything with its saline showers. There is a story told about a rabbit-trapper who happened to be on the Great Saltee during a gale and who could not leave the old farmhouse, half a mile from the cliffs, because of the intensity of the sheets of spray from the lashing waves.

It is possible that the Saltees derived their name from the salty spray and spume that so often baptises the two islands.

An old photograph of the Hook lighthouse. It is believed to be the oldest in Europe; the tower is over 750 years old and a warning light was kept here by monks from the 5th century.

FOOTNOTES – CHAPTER 2

1. "In Ireland we find our oldest rocks at Rosslare and Kilmore Quay in Wexford, and these have been given an age of 2,000 million years; elsewhere in the world still older rocks are known" – Prof. Frank Mitchell in *The Irish Landscape,* Collins (1976).

2. "Fossils made their first appearance in abundance about 600 million years ago, and fossiliferous deposits of this age occur in Wales. These rocks have been named Cambrian, and the archaic forms of life represented by the fossils are called Palaeozoic. The vast majority of still older rocks have either no fossils, or only a very limited range of them, and have so far largely defeated all attempts to sort them out. In despair geologists have lumped them together under the simple name of Pre-Cambrian, even though the period of time they represent is immensely long" – *The Irish Landscape.*

3. The names of the natural features of the islands are a mixture of Irish, English and Yola (the old Forth and Bargy dialect). "Makeston", for example, is the "makes' stone", "Makes" being the local name for kittiwakes. The rock is a favourite roosting-place for kittiwakes.

4. Neamestown may have been the ancestral home of the Neames, later prominent in Kent. But is the name, perhaps, a corruption of "Naomh's town", the saint's town – a link with St. Patrick? Besides St. Patrick's Bridge, there is St. Patrick's Well, a fresh-water spring near Grange. Local people will tell you that stones removed from St. Patrick's Bridge find their way back to it, overnight. There is a story about a man who used some stones from the Bridge to build a house far inland, in defiance of tradition. The house unaccountably fell without warning. The late John Parle, of the Great Saltee, used a large slab from St. Patrick's Bridge as a headstone for the family burial plot in Killag graveyard.

5. In *Explanatory Memoir of the Geological Survey of Ireland,* 1879.

6. See also Samuel Lewis, *Topographical Dictionary of Ireland,* 1837: "A late return from the resident incumbent of the adjoining parish on the mainland states that these islands are considered to form part of the County of Tipperary."

7. *Chronicles of the County Wexford,* compiled by George Griffiths, editor of the Co. Wexford Almanac and Directory, 1877.

8. St. Patrick's Bridge should not be confused with "St. Patrick's Ridge", which was a ridge of corn specially grown by tenants and donated to landlords in medieval times in lieu of service. As the Church held so much of the land in those days, the religious title "St. Patrick's Ridges" was applied to the plots. See William Monck Mason, *Hibernia Antiqua et Hodierna* (1819), footnotes t and u, pages 71, Book 1.

9. *The Way that I went,* by R. L. Praeger, Methuen 1937, Allen Figgis Dublin 1969.

The Saltees are one of the main breeding areas for Grey Seals. There are more than 40 animals there now. This Seal is sometimes referred to as the Atlantic Grey Seal.

Chapter 3
Earliest Times

We cannot be certain as to when man first lived on the Saltees, but from traces of habitation there we can fix approximate dates for periods of residence by early settlers.

As long ago as 3,500 to 2,000 B.C. there were probably people on the islands. This has been deduced from the discovery, on the Great Saltee in 1957, of a crude flint,[1] dating from the Neolithic Period. This leaf-shaped flake of flint, resembling what archaeologists call a "Bann flake",[2] was probably used by New Stone Age man, the first known inhabitant of the Saltees.

The islands offered many advantages to a nomadic tribe — a temperate climate, safety from enemies and wild animals,[3] good fishing, fertile soil and an abundance of shell-fish, seabirds and seabirds' eggs.[4]

The Neolithic way of life included cultivated crops, domesticated animals, pottery and stone implements. Neolithic man lived in crude shelters of branches and mud, or in caves. He had skin-covered, currach-type boats in which he could transport his cattle and sheep, trussed and lying on their sides. Cattle, horses and sheep were carried thus, to and from the Saltees, well into the 20th century.

What looks like an ancient grave, of indeterminate age and origin, is situated midway on the saddle between the two highest points of the Great Saltee. This consists of several large stone slabs, set on edge, similar to the support stones of dolmens.

Even without a cap-stone, this formation of slabs has counterparts in many other places in Ireland and most of these have been classified as "gallery graves" or "cist graves".

There is more tangible evidence of later habitation on the Great Saltee. These include a promontory fort, circular rath-like configurations, discovered recently and apparently overlooked previously, and traces of rectangular foundations where a building once stood.

The promontory fort, identified in the summer of 1976, by Prof. Frank Mitchell and Dr. Edward Culleton, stands on the northmost foreland of the

Above – Two great stones of what may have been a cist grave, on the Great Saltee.

Right – An artist's impression of the Saltee Ogham stone as it may have stood originally.

Below – A unique photograph, from the Mason collection, showing the Saltee Ogham stone lying in its original setting on the Great Saltee.

Great Saltee, overlooking what is called Sebber Bridge.[5] On the ground traces are not easily discernible, but an aerial photograph shows clearly the outline of the fort with its curved perimeter defending the headland.

What little trace there is to be detected on the ground consists of broken sections of what may have been an earthen rampart across the point. The area inside the perimeter rampart is now small but this may be due to the considerable erosion of Sebber Point. Excavation — and none has been carried out on the Saltees — might well confirm this as a promontory fort of the Early Iron Age[6] (500 B.C. to 500 A.D.). Since the site must be relatively undisturbed finds there could be significant, and could tell us much more about the island inhabitants in those far-off days.

Of equal interest are the traces of what appear to be ring-forts and circular dwellings which the author first discovered while examining an aerial photograph of the Great Saltee taken in 1952. These unusual configurations appear to have escaped the attention of surveyors and archaeologists up to now. Again excavation or closer examination could reveal vital links in the chain of human habitation on the Saltees.

The two biggest configurations are semi-circles merging into each other in an area called "The Ace of Diamonds". On the ground they are not noticeable but the aerial photograph clearly shows the partial rings at a time when there was less under-growth and bracken and fewer weeds.

There are three or four smaller circles and they are situated beside what is appropriately, and significantly perhaps, called "The Ring Field",[7] at the foot of the southern bluffs of the Great Saltee. It is a sheltered place, with a well (Frenchman's Well) only a short distance away; in short one of the most suitable places for dwellings on the island.

Again, bracken and weeds now obscure traces of these rings at ground-level. Excavation is probably the only way to determine what they are. Radio carbon dating of tools, bones, charcoal and other possible finds could fix the time of their construction and habitation. They may well be the foundations of clochans and could represent the period of Celtic invasion and settlement, which started about 600 B.C.

There are further pieces of evidence of human presence on the islands and these point to the Early Christian era (4th to 8th century A.D.). They comprise a name, some foundations and an Ogham stone. The name is "The Abbey Field", a cleared area adjoining the promontory fort overlooking Sebber Bridge.

If there was an abbey or monastery here little visible trace now remains. Yet at certain times of the year, in early Spring or very late Autumn, one can make out a rectangular shape, suggesting the foundations of a building, in the sward underfoot. Is this the site of a small monastery or abbey? The name "Abbey Field" suggests something of the sort. Lewis, in his *Topographical Dictionary of Ireland*, states: "On the eastern extremity, still called the Abbey Point, are the ruins of a building supposed to have been a religious house". In Lewis's time (early 19th century) there were obviously ruins there, but these remains have since disappeared.

Bassett, who wrote his *Guide and Directory to Co. Wexford* some years later (1885), refers to "a strip known as the Abbey" but adds that there were no

23

KEY (Section of Gt. Saltee)

1 = Possible cist grave
2 = Site of "throne" and obelisk
3 = "Ace of Diamonds" showing
    traces of ring forts.
4 = Farmhouse
5 = Remains of duck pond.
6 = Haggard, with corn stands.
7 = Farm buildings (inc. forge).
8 = Cottage
9 = Site of dried-up lake.
10 = Old road.
11 = Airstrip
12 = "Royal Mile"
13 = Big Tommeen
14 = Small Tommeen
15 = Sod Rock.
16 = "Sandy Burrow"
17 = Fulmar Bay

Bottom left — An enlargement of part of an aerial photograph of the Great Saltee, showing the broken earthwork of a promontory fort on Sebber Point.

Bottom right — The Saltees flint. It measures 3.09 cm (length), 2.4 cm (width) and 4.09 mm (thickness).

foundations visible in his day.

Traces of a rectangular building overlooking the Ring are probably the remains of a house built to store boat-gear — the Ring being the only possible mooring place on the Great Saltee. The island cot (boat) was kept there during the occupancy of the island by Claude Francis between 1939 and 1943. Mr. Francis, of Rathjarney, Killinick, Co. Wexford, farmed the bigger island successfully during those years, producing fine crops of early potatoes and also cereals. He was the last settled inhabitant of the islands.

On the Little Saltee, too, probable traces of early habitation have been found.[8] On the northern tip close to the edge of the low cliff, numerous human bones were found some years ago by a Kilmore Quay fisherman. He noticed at the time an unusual number of small bones, "like fingers and foot bones," he told me. He re-interred them all in a convenient rabbit-burrow. Legend has a name for this place: it is called the Giant's Grave, and there are stories of frightened and snorting plough-horses stopping short of it and refusing to go near it when the field was being ploughed in former times.

But there is more tangible evidence in the Ogham stone which was found on the Great Saltee in the early 1930s. R.A.S. Macalister[9] describes it thus:

"A waterworn pulvinar of grit, 2'9" x 0'9" x 0'8½", inscribed in two lines of Ogham pocked on the curved sides: LONAMNI AVI BARI.[10] The A in the first word, and the A as well as l ^{1234} in the second are worn or battered away. This inscription was discovered on the Great Saltee by Mr. Standish Mason, of Dublin. It was afterwards removed by some persons, apparently induced by hope of gain inspired by publication in a local newspaper; but the rising of a gale so frightened the speculators that they threw it into the sea — fortunately not into deep water, for it was subsequently rescued and brought to the mainland: When I saw it (April 2, 1937) it was in the custody of the Parish Priest of Piercestown".

The Ogham stone is now in the County Museum in Enniscorthy Castle with the following addendum to Macalister's description on a framed note: "The late Father Joseph Ranson[11] said this account was not true; that Fr. Tomas O'Byrne, P.P., Piercestown, took the stone from the island to preserve it, that the stone fell into the water by accident while putting it on boat".

There is, apparently, an element of truth in both accounts. The existence of the Ogham stone on the Great Saltee was common knowledge in the Kilmore area for many years and it had stood there, in what may have been its original position near the farmhouse, untouched through generations. In the early 1920s, however, a feud developed between two local men, each of whom claimed the stone as his property. There was, as Macalister infers, a suggestion that the stone might be valuable and that its possessor might be financially rewarded for handing it over to the proper authority. A petty game of hide-and-seek ensued, with one man hiding the stone and the other searching the island until he eventually found it — and hid it in turn. This "diversion" went on for some time, until a third person stepped in, made a pact with the man who then knew where the stone was hidden, and attempted to take it off the island. It was during this attempt, the story goes, that the stone fell into the sea while being loaded on to a boat. It lay in fairly shallow water for some years until recovered and given into the safe keeping of Father O'Byrne.

Macalister does not give any explanation of the inscription on the Great Saltee Ogham stone. Most Ogham plinths date from the Early Christian period and are believed to mark the graves of hermits, chieftains or scribes. The Saltee stone may well have fulfilled this function, standing for centuries over the last resting-place of the remains of an island monk or anchorite.

It is one positive piece of evidence, at any rate, that the Great Saltee was inhabited, albeit by a few hermits, sometime between the 4th and 8th centuries. The first Norse raids on the Irish coast took place in 795 A.D.[12] — the beginning of one era and the end of another — even for the Saltees, perhaps.

FOOTNOTES – CHAPTER 3

1. Now in the National Museum, Dublin. A museum official says it is definitely man-made but cannot be classified as a particular type of implement. It may well be a waste product of flint-working.

2. "Bann Flakes" are so-called because of the great numbers found beside the river Bann, south of Coleraine. It is here that the earliest record of man in Ireland has recently been confirmed, dated by radio carbon to between 8,700 and 8,600 years ago.

3. The wild animals feared by man in Ireland in these times were the wolf, bear and wild boar.

4. The plentiful rabbits found on the Saltees are a comparatively recent introduction. The Anglo-Normans brought the rabbit to Ireland.

5. Sebber or Sever Bridge appears to be the beginning of a smaller tidal bar or glacial moraine similar to St. Patrick's Bridge. Does the name derive from St. Ibar, also pronounced locally as St. Ivor, and denote local insistence on honouring the Wexford saint, just as the bigger "bridge" honours St. Patrick?

6. The Sebber Bridge promontory fort seems to fulfil the requirements of such structures as outlined by Dr. Sean P. O'Riordain in his *Antiquities of the Irish Countryside:* "Economy of effort in the enclosing of a large area is achieved by building the defence across the narrow neck of a sea-girt promontory".

7. "The Ring Field" could also be called after the Ring, a curved arm of shingle enclosing a tidal lagoon, which the field overlooks. From *rinn,* Irish for headland.

8. It has also been suggested that the bones found in the "Giant's Grave" are those of ship-wrecked sailors drowned when their vessel ran on to hidden rocks near the tip of the Little Saltee.

9. Macalister: *Corpus Inscriptionum,* 1,48. Ogham is an early Irish form of writing, the letters being represented by lines up to five in number written above, below or across a stem line. On Ogham stones one or more of the corners is utilised as a stem line — O'Riordain.

10. An official of the National Museum, Dublin, has suggested that the inscription LONAMNI AVI BARI may derive from "Lonam Ui Bhairr", being the genitive case, the word "Cloch" (Stone) being understood at the beginning. Thus "Cloch Lonam Ui Bhairr", the Stone of Lonan of Barr, theorising that "Lonamni" should read "Lonagni", being rendered thus because of erosion. We are still left with the question: Who was Lonan? And was he of Bargy, Ui Bhairrce, perhaps?

11. Rev. Joseph Ranson, C.C., Enniscorthy, one of Wexford's most noted historians and antiquarians. Chiefly responsible for the setting-up of the County Museum in Enniscorthy Castle, and probably best remembered for his collection of *Songs of the Wexford Coast.* He died in 1964.

12. *An account of the Danes and Norwegians in England, Scotland and Ireland,* by J. J. A. Worsaae, (John Murray, London, 1852).

Chapter 4
Names

If the Saltees had any other name before their present title, it has been lost for ever. No record, written or oral, exists of a name in the Irish language, although it can be presumed that the islands had an ancient name, since they were inhabited from a very early period.

There is an Irish version of the present name, Na Saltaeisi,[1] but this appears to be merely a Gaelicisation of "The Saltees" and not an original name in itself. The first written form of the present name is found on an early Italian map of Ireland dating from 1327-1339.[2] On this chart it is rendered "Saltis", while other versions such as "Saliez" and "Saltei" are found on other Italian maps dated 1426, 1450, 1544 and 1552.[3] On a further map of the year 1500 the name is given in Spanish as "Y de Sallos", which is a condensation of "Ysla de Sallos", the last word probably being a mis-spelling of "Saltos".

Progressing through the centuries, we find further versions of the name on maps of Ireland and Britain: "Salteis" (c.1534),[4] "Saltes (1560,[5] c.1600[6] and 1610[7]), while another, obviously corrupted, form ("The Salters") is found in State papers[8] of the years 1603-28. A schedule of lands dating from about 1648 gives the information that "Salt Isles" were "waste",[9] while the current name "Saltees" is found in a maritime survey of 1776.[10] Other old forms of the name, for example "Shalts", "Shast" and "Saltushe", are merely corruptions and probably originated through mis-spelling, bad pronunciation or translation from ancient deeds and documents.

As for the origin of the name "Saltees" itself, there are two theories — that the name is of Norse or of Old or Middle English derivation. The name Saltee immediately suggests a Norse origin (Salt ey, meaning salt island), deriving from the phenomenon of the salt spray which showers across the islands at times of high wind and waves. Norse names abound along this part of the Wexford coastline— Tuskar,[11] Greenore, Carnsore,[12] Selskar,[13] Skar[14] and Wexford itself, all evidence of the presence and influence here of Viking sea-raiders whose long-boats sailed these waters, first as plunderers, ultimately as traders.

Since the Saltees are among the most prominent features of this sea-area, it is most likely that the Norse named the dangerous, spray-drenched islands as

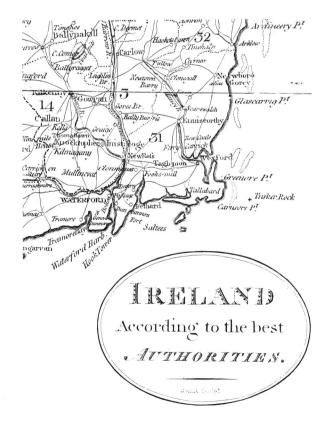

Many old maps erred badly in their location and numbering of the Saltees. The Elizabethan era map (above), for example, does not show the Saltees at all.

Another map first published in Waghenaer's chart collection, 1596/1597 and reproduced here (top left) from the French edition of the collection, 1600, shows THREE islands called *Saltes*. The mystery of the third Saltee island deepens when one consults Sir Richard Griffith's *First Valuation of Ireland* (Leinster, 1844) and finds this reference to a third island: "... a small island of no agricultural value containing 1 rood and 8 perches." The "Valuation" of 1853 gives Susan Boxwell as tenant and John Rowe as lessor of this mystery isle.

A third island is also shown in the map reproduced in *Topographica Hibernica*, by Wm. M. Seward (Dublin, 1795) and referred to in the text (below) What has happened to this third island?

them in their aprons. At high water the fall is hardly 3 feet, and. then the fish swim up that easy acclivity without leaping.

SALT, a bar. in co. Kildare, prev. Leinster.

SALTEES, three islands on the coast of the bar. Bargie, co. Wexford, prov. Leinster, fit. about a league from the shore. Lat. 52 : 10, lon. 6 : 30.

early as the 9th or 10th century. The islands were on the sea-route between the Norse ports of Waterford and Wexford, and could also be seen from many points in the Barony of Forth wherein lay "the cantred of the Ostmen"[15]

Praeger[16] says the name Saltee is derived from the Danish "salt oe"[17] (salt island) but this is modern Danish and not at all old enough to explain its application to the islands as far back as the 14th century. An Old or Middle English origin ("salt-ie") would be more likely than a modern English one, especially since Old English (to about 1100) and Middle English (1110 to 1500) are closely related to Norse. Of the two choices, Norse or Old/Middle English, I favour the former.

The incidence of many other Norse names in the region is a telling factor, suggesting Norse familiarity with the whole coastal area and its contiguous seas and islands; it would be most unlikely that these experienced sea-farers would overlook the navigational hazards of the islands by leaving them un-named; and the name itself was apparently already well-established and widely known as early as 1327.

Further, a study of Norman documents shows that these later colonisers seemingly adopted the name Saltees, a pointer surely to the probability that the name as such was in use as far back as 1169. Altogether the case for a Norse origin is a strong one.

If the Vikings gave us the name by which the Saltees have since been known, and may even have had a settlement on the islands, they were not by any means the first to live there. There is evidence of much earlier habitation, especially on the Great Saltee.

FOOTNOTES – CHAPTER 4

1. Irish version from Ring, Co. Waterford (on tape).

2. Westropp:*Early Italian maps of Ireland.* Proceedings of the Royal Irish Academy, *xxx, 421.*

3. Westropp, as above.

4. Early maps of the British Isles. British Museum Cotton ms., aug. i.i.f.9.

5. Ortelius', map, as above.

6. Baptista Boazio's map, T.C.D. ms. (1209.83).

7. Speed's map, as above.

8. *Calendar State Papers,* Carew, 1603-28, p.438.

9. A schedule of lands, c.1648. See Hore, IV, 188.

10. Mackenzie: *Maritime Survey,* 1776.

11. The ending "skar" is from "sker" or "skjaer", Norse for reef or rock.

12. The ending "ore" is from ore, Norse for "sandy point of a promontory". Carn means mound.

13. A rock in Bannow Bay, "seal's rock". Kilmore Quay fishermen pronounce "seal" as "sell".

14. The Skar estuary which opens into Bannow Bay. Also a rocky eminence at Scar, Duncormick.

15. The cantred, or territory, of the Ostmen (Norse) in Wexford comprised the eastern part of the Barony of Forth, stretching along the coast from Wexford to Rosslare.

16. R. L. Praeger, *The Way that I went.*

17. Compare "Keeroe" or "Keroe", versions of Keeragh, the name of two small islands off Cullens-town. "Martin Doyle" (Rev. William Hickey) refers to the "Keroe Islands" in his *Notes and Gleanings relating to the County of Wexford.* He also states that "Wexford, Bargie, Forth, Scar, Tuscar, Saltees and Slaney, are among the names given by the Danes previously to the immigration of the first English settlers" (p.3.). Joyce, *Irish Names of Places* says that the Irish version of Keeragh is Oilean na gCaorach, or Island of the Sheep. It has been suggested to me that Saltee may derive from the Norse word "Saud" (meaning sheep) and "ey" (island) — again, sheep island.

Chapter 5
Medieval Times

There are no contemporary records relating to the history of the Saltees until we reach the 13th century. It is by no means certain if the islands continued to be inhabited during the greater part of those turbulent intervening centuries.

Undoubtedly the Saltees attracted the attention of the first marauding Vikings and probably figured on the first crude charts of these hardy navigators; just as probable was their inclusion on the maps of the Norman adventurers who passed close to the islands on that May day in 1169 when the first mailed warriors waded ashore on Bannow Island.[1] But of recorded reference to the Saltees there is none until we reach the middle of the 13th century. Over the years between it is likely that the islands had their own little communities of farmers and fishermen, living frugally but at least safely while other parts of the country suffered the ravages of Norse raids, Irish inter-tribal warfare, Anglo-Norman incursions and attempts at the complete sub-jugation of Ireland.

As the dominion of the Anglo-Normans was extended, and with it the growth of state and church bureaucracy and records, we begin to find references to the Saltees in the English State papers and church documents.

Probably the first of these references is found in a deed of 1245[2] by which the Saltees and the Island of Bannow were granted to the Abbot and monks of Tintern Abbey. The lease, incidentally, was perpetual and the rent ten marks[3] a year. This deed reads as follows:

"Be it known that we have granted, conceded, etc. to the Abbot and Convent of De Voto, all the lands and all the town and country property which we possessed and held hitherto in Ireland from the gift in pious memory of that late nobleman, Hervey de Monte Maurice, which lands are as follows – the whole of our land of Kilmore, of Kenture and of Banewe..... with the island of Bannow and the two islands of Saheye (recte Salteye)...."[4]

The grantors in this case were the Abbot and monks of Canterbury in England, who had been given possession of these lands through the bequest of Hervey de Monte Marisco (or Montmorency, or Monte Maurice). Hervey, who had accompanied his nephew Strongbow[5] in the Norman invasion of Ireland,

Above – The Oseberg ship, a typical Viking vessel, now preserved in a museum.

Top – A reproduction of a section of the first deed of Tintern Abbey, 1245, with its reference (line 15) to "duas insulas de Salteya".

had been granted a large tract of land in south Wexford by Dermot Mac Murrough. Hervey bestowed much of the land upon Christ Church, Canterbury, and its monks who, however, as absentee landlords, could get no rents.

The Canterbury monks in turn leased the lands to the resident monks of Tintern Abbey in 1245 at an annual rent of £4.6s.8d. In 1318 the Tintern Abbey monks redeemed this rent by a payment of £100 — more than twenty years' purchase of the same.[6] Included in the lands were the Saltees.

For the next two hundred years the islands must have remained among the possessions of the Tintern community and were, apparently, inhabited by Anglo-Norman tenant-farmers and fishermen — and, perhaps, by a small community of monks. In 1533, the next time we find a reference to them in old records, the islands were still in the hands of the Abbot of Tintern. In that year the Abbot granted to James Keating the lease of part of the "Lytyll Salteis" and half of the "Common Causeway" at a rental of 3s. 4d., to be paid half-yearly.[7]

This is the first reference to the "Common Causeway" and the first recorded evidence that St. Patrick's Bridge was usable as a causeway to get to and from the Little Saltee.

The fact that James Keating was willing to pay a rent for part of St. Patrick's Bridge suggests that it had a use; the name "Common Causeway" suggests the manner in which it was used — as a traversible route from the mainland to the Little Saltee, most likely at low tide. In those days the rounded boulders which form the foundation of the ridge were probably covered with shingle, as is the landward end at Neamestown today, thus making it easier for man and animal to negotiate. Indeed, it is possible that the lessees of the "Common Causeway" were required to keep it in usable condition for the common good, by replacing stones and shingle washed away by the tide.[8]

Then 1538 came, and with it the dissolution of the abbeys by Henry VIII. Among them was Tintern which, with its estates, passed into the king's hands. He granted them to his Seneschal for Co. Wexford, William Seyntlo of Rosegarland.[9] The grant relating to this transference, dated January 27, 1538, reads in part as follows:

"....the islands called the Salteys... with all the buildings, titles, profits, etc. to the same islands.... belonging.... and the rectory of Kilmore, parcel of the possessions of the Abbey of Tynterne by a lease dated 20th December, 1529, for 21 years, to said William, being surrendered, to hold for life, by fealty only".

But, only two years later, on January 28, 1540, the same William was writing to Secretary Cromwell[10] that "he cannot pay the tithes of Kilmore which had belonged to the Abbey of Tinern, and that the soldiers allowed him had been withdrawn and therefore he could not protect the county from the continual spoils, burnings and destruction wrought by the Kavanaghs".

In an inquisition of the year 1540 the "manorlands of Shast" (Saltees) are listed: there were "120 acres of arable, meadow, pasture and wood" on the bigger islands, and "60 acres of the same mixture" on the Little Saltee. A further inquisition, in 1543, described the Saltees as "Saltushe, an island within the sea", containing in all one hundred and eighty acres of pasture, arable land, meadow and wood. This description, although mentioning only one island, seems to include the two Saltees (120 + 60 acres = 180).

It is interesting to note the reference to woods. Obviously there must have been numerous trees on the islands in those days — the remains of post-glacial forests, perhaps. The absence of other forms of fuel, however, soon resulted in all the trees being used as firewood, leaving the islands denuded. More recently, in this century, a fresh attempt has been made to re-introduce trees on the Great Saltee but only a few stunted sycamores bear witness to this. The present owner, Michael Neale, has planted avenues of cordyline (commonly called palm) which appear to be surviving.

Another inquisition, dated August 30th, 1544, found one hundred and twenty acres in "Shalts" (yet another corruption of "Saltees"). The annual value, besides reprises, of these one hundred and twenty acres was 10s., while the sixty acres "in the other townland of Shalts" were valued, besides reprises, at 6s. 8d. Two years later the "Salt Iles" were described as "waste" — a term that could cover several possibilities, e.g. unoccupied land, poor land, or devastated areas. It is possible that, in the turmoil of the times, the islands were evacuated temporarily and the land was left uncared-for. Whatever their fate, in 1548 the Saltees, among other lands, were leased to John Isham, of Bryanstown, Seneschal of Co. Wexford.

Six years later, in 1554, we find [11] "the two islands called the Saltees, parcel of the possessions of the late Abbey, in the hands of the Crown, and William Browne, of Mulranken,[12] accused of entry and intrusion".

Soon afterwards, Tintern and its lands were granted to Captain Anthony Colclough,[13] of Staffordshire. Commander of the King's guards, he had been stationed in Leighlin-Bridge, Co. Carlow, and took up residence at Tintern in 1562. He leased some of the lands, including the Saltees, to a Thomas Wood in 1566, for 40 years, and Wood's tenure brings us into another, more exciting, era in the story of the Saltees.

Tintern Abbey, Co. Wexford, whose community of monks were granted the Saltees in the 13th century.

FOOTNOTES – CHAPTER 5

1. "The Song of Dermot and the Earl" says the first invaders landed "a la Banne"; Giraldus Cambrensis, "apud Banuam"; a deed of 1175 relating to the granting of lands by Hervey de Monte Marisco to Christ Church, Canterbury, refers to "insula de Banewe" (the island of Bannow). It is no longer an island, drifting sand having filled in the old shipping channel. (see my *Norman Invasion of Ireland,* Anvil Books, 1970).

2. The deed referred to here, dated 1245, is in Cambridge University Library, England, in the Registry of Henry, Prior of Christ Church, Canterbury. The text is in abbreviated Latin.

3. A mark was the equivalent of thirteen shillings and four pence (old currency).

4. "Convent of De Voto" or "of the Vow", i.e. Tintern which was founded by William Marshall, Earl of Pembroke, in 1200, as a result of a vow made during a stormy sea-crossing from Wales to Ireland. He vowed that if he, his wife and crew were saved he would found a monastery in thanksgiving. The ship was driven ashore in Bannow Bay and all aboard were saved. William brought over Cistercians from the mother-house at Tintern in Monmouthshire, Wales, to form the Co. Wexford "De Voto" community.

5. Hervey de Monte Marisco was Seneschal or Chief Steward of all the lands acquired by Strongbow. He was a curious mixture of soldier, adventurer and church benefactor — as indeed were many of the Cambro-Normans. He later resigned his stewardship, became a monk and joined the Cistercian community at Dunbrody. He died there in 1205 at the age of seventy-five. In the church of Dunbrody Abbey, in a niche near the high altar, Hervey's ornate burial monument, of black marble, stood until 1798 when a party of soldiers from Duncannon Fort wantonly destroyed it.

6. Prof. G. T. Stokes, D.D. in *Ireland and the Anglo Norman Church,* p.74, footnote 1.

7. Lease dated Jan. 10, 1533. Copied from Memoranda Rolls of the Exchequer, Ireland, by P. H. Hore. Strangely, one of the last people to use the "Common Causeway" was also a man named Keating, the great-grandfather of Mr. James Keating of Tenacre. He recalled driving cattle across the "Causeway" about 1840. Bassett, in his 1885 *Directory* of Co. Wexford, says of the Bridge: "As a walk it is difficult — but apparently possible".

8. There has obviously been considerable erosion of St. Patrick's Bridge. Apart from the stories handed down in Kilmore area about people walking dry-footed to the Little Saltee, there is the fact that St. Patrick's Rock, now surrounded by water even at low tide, was sixty years ago almost on dry land at ebb-tide. P. H. Hore, in his *History of Co. Wexford* mentions that "the Bridge is *now* covered with many feet of water even at low tide". His history was written at the end of the 19th century. The "Tintern" volume was published in 1901.

6. Seyntlo, variously rendered as St. Lo, St. Loo and Saintlo, was granted the lands of the Nevilles at Rosegarland. It was later (as it still is) the home of the Leigh family, of whom the chronicler Robert Leigh (1684) was a noted member.

10. Thomas Cromwell (1485?-1540), chief minister and adviser to Henry VIII. He was eventually made Earl of Essex and later beheaded after falling into disfavour with Henry.

11. Mem. Rot. Hib. 1-2, Philip and Mary, No.43. Public Record Office, Dublin. It should be mentioned that most of the ancient deeds, grants and inquisitions mentioned in this chapter were destroyed in the Four Courts conflagration in 1922. Fortunately they had been already copied by Philip Herbert Hore, the Wexford historian, and their translations are to be found in his monumental *History of the Town and County of Wexford.*

12. Mulrankan, now Mulrankin, near Bridgetown, Bargy. This was the ancestral home of the Brownes. The castle, called Rathronan Castle, is still occupied by descendants of the Brownes

13. Anthony Colclough, knighted in 1581-82, had seven sons who married into leading Anglo-Irish families. He died in 1584 and is buried in the chapel of Tintern Abbey. The Colcloughs (pronounced Coakleys) held Tintern until 1958 when the last member of the family to reside at Tintern Abbey, Miss Lucy Wilmot Maria Susanna Biddulph Colclough, presented the Abbey to the Irish nation, but retained the lands. The Board of Works is currently engaged on a programme of repair and reconstruction on the beautiful old buildings. Miss Colclough, aged 87 at the time of writing, now resides at nearby Tintern House, Saltmills.

Chapter 6
Pirates and Smugglers

The 16th, 17th and 18th centuries saw a vast expansion in international trade, in tremendous voyages of discovery, in exploration of new lands and in finding of new wealth. All this was concurrent with a similar growth in trade between Tudor England, Ireland, the Indies, and the Americas. Long voyages and rich cargoes called for bigger and better ships and the era of the mighty merchant-man was ushered in. These capacious vessels sailed home to English ports with holds packed with the riches of the newly-discovered lands — wines, rum, silk, spices, gold, silver, precious stones, furs, ivory, sugar, cotton.

Inevitably all this sea-borne wealth attracted pirates, smugglers and wreckers. The pirates began to capture and plunder the richly-laden merchantmen in the busy sea-lanes off the south coast of Ireland. Here, in what is now called the Celtic Sea, were the crowded routes to the Bristol Channel and St. George's Channel leading to some of the great trading ports of England, Wales and Ireland — Bristol, Cardiff, Liverpool, Waterford, Dublin and Belfast.

A glance at a map shows how the Saltees dominated these sea-approaches and how ideally they were situated as a base for pirates. Indeed the entire south coast of Wexford presented so many hazards to the mariner and sea-trader that its reputation became notorious. There were the ever-present dangers of the perilous coast-line from the Hook to Tuskar — one of the worst stretches of reefs, rocks, shoals and islands to be found anywhere in western Europe.[1] Add to those, fierce tidal currents[2] that swept helpless vessels to their doom on the shallows and beaches of Ballyteigue Bay, out of which, in the days of sail, there was no escape in a southerly or south-westerly gale.

But the natural hazards of storms, rocks and tides were not the only ones besetting sea-farers in this area. There were, as already mentioned, the wreckers, the plunderers and the pirates.

The wrecking or plundering of ships is nothing new along the coast of Ireland, any more than it is in places such as Cornwall, Pembrokeshire or the Hebrides. For hundreds of years coastal residents in these parts have regarded it as their right to plunder a ship after saving its occupants. As recently as 1934, the owner of a ship stranded off the Donegal coast claimed damages in

36

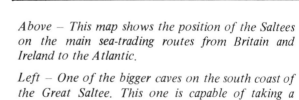

Above – This map shows the position of the Saltees on the main sea-trading routes from Britain and Ireland to the Atlantic.

Left – One of the bigger caves on the south coast of the Great Saltee. This one is capable of taking a lugger at high water.

court from the County Council and was awarded £660 compensation for the plundering of his vessel.

There are numerous descriptions of the plundering of ships on the south Wexford coast. Some of these vessels were wrecked or driven ashore in storms; others, it must be said, were lured to their doom by wreckers. This usually happened at night when cunningly manipulated lights on cliff-tops led skippers to believe they were following other ships in safe waters.

A common practice was to tie a lighted lantern to the horns of a grazing cow. From the deck of a ship near the coast the bobbing lantern looked like the riding light of a ship at sea. By the time the captain of the lured ship realised his mistake it was too late, and his vessel ended on the rocks or the strand, another victim for the wreckers and plunderers.

An article in *The People*, Wexford's weekly paper, of September 15, 1950, gives the following description of the situation as an observer in south Wexford saw it in the early 1800s:

"In the early years of the century, some coastal inhabitants of Carne, in Co. Wexford, were reputed to make considerable money from ship-wrecks. Although the people did everything possible to save lives, they considered they had a claim, by user from past times, to take as compensation for their help all the cargo and gear, including the effects of the sailors, and the fittings of the ships so wrecked. Shipwrecks were frequent off this dangerous coast until the erection of the lighthouse on Tuskar Rock mitigated such dreadful occurrences. Dick Barry of Balleconnor Castle, credited to be the first man who successfully resisted the payment of toll on entering the Wexford market with goods, once gave an interviewer a shocking description of the avidity with which persons, of both sexes, rushed down to the rocks when a vessel, in sight, was expected to be wrecked; he recalled their frantic exclamations that such might be her fate, invoking even particular rocks on which she was likely to strike to "claim the wreck", and of their imprecations when the beleagured ship was so fortunate to disappoint their expectations of the spoil".

Nor was this behaviour a 19th-century phenomenon. In January, 1549, we find the Mayor of Limerick complaining to Lord Deputy Bellingham that a ship belonging to that port (Limerick), on her voyage from Spain to that city with a cargo of wine, was wrecked off the south Wexford coast and plundered by the inhabitants.[3]

About 1630, as P. H. Hore relates,[4] "there were reports of several wrecks on the coast, and complaints that although endeavours to save the crews of these vessels were made, the inhabitants of Forth and Bargy took possession of the cargo and contents of all casks, etc., which came ashore, and claimed jetsam and flotsam as their right".

Hore continues: "Pirates also infested the coast and, according to the complaints made to the Lords of the Privy Council in England, obtained either by cajolery or intimidation supplies from the inhabitants. They used the caves of the Saltees as a storehouse for their ill-gotten gains."

One of the most notorious of these 16th and 17th century pirates was Alexander Vailes and the State papers of the year 1587 contain numerous complaints to the Lord Deputy and the Privy Council of the many and grievous losses sustained by the merchant traders of Ross and Waterford, and foreign trading vessels entering and leaving the Haven by organised bands of pirates who infested the sea-lanes off the south-east coast of Ireland.

Correspondence about Vailes complains that he boarded a French ship opposite Duncannon Fort in the Suir-Barrow estuary and pillaged "46 tonnes of wynes which was presently brought by the said pyrates to Waterford and there sould to the inhabitants thereof, and other places thereabouts".

Vaile's impudence apparently matched his daring. Anyone who could pillage a cargo of wine under the guns of Duncannon Fort deserved the admiration and aid of many of the coastal inhabitants. Such, indeed, was the case. Not only were the pirates popular with the local people (after all both had a common enemy in the English)[5] but the freebooters also did a considerable illegal trade with the local gentry who were accused of harbouring "dyvars pyrates and of receiving part of the goods robbed by them and stowlen within the haven of Waterford".

The authorities were convinced, in fact, that many of the cellars of castles in Co. Wexford, especially those near the south coast, were stocked with brandy and wine supplied by pirates from the Saltees, and suspected gentry were required to take out bonds to the effect that they would not "aide, relieve or maintain any such pyrates or in any way inter-meddle with them".

There is voluminous correspondence in the State Papers of this period dealing with the depredations of pirates on merchant shipping off the east and south coasts of Ireland. It is stated that ships could hardly put out from Dublin, Wicklow, Wexford or Waterford, without being in danger of capture. Hore gives the following extract from a letter from Captain Richard Plumleigh, to the Lords of the Admiralty, dated September 2, 1632:

"I have had the chase of 2 or 3 Biskayners about the Saltees and have pursued them into shold (shallow) waters and home to the very Rocks; that by such rough dealing with them they may be advised to forbeare troubling the trade of this Kingdom and pillaging the poore Fishermen upon the coast." [6]

The Saltees were recognised as a base for the pirates. The late Dr. George Hadden, historian, Wexford, discussed this subject with me some years before his death in 1974. He said: "There are many records of pirates based on the Saltees. The islands would be difficult to approach and would be admirably placed across the entrances to all the trade-ports of the Irish Sea from the south. The difficulty of approach by Government gunboats was increased by the fact that the coastal folk were at outs with the power across the water. Also it was a dangerous coast for those not acquainted with its currents".

Dr. Hadden also listed the disadvantages of the Saltees base: "The islands are a place of storms, there is no harbour, no roadstead, no shelter; no place a ship could rest, much less where she could be careened for painting or re-fitting. They could get water — perhaps they did. They could even bury treasure — but even legend has no tale of it. At best they could cache ammunition and stores and perhaps have a village of pirate homes where men might take an occasional turn ashore — particularly if they were local men, outlawed only while they were actually "on business". Yes, if we care to invest the Saltees with the glamour of Treasure Island, why should we not?"

Although there are numerous caves on the Saltees where pirates could have stored booty or cached stores, there are no legends or traditions about hidden treasure on the islands. Many of the caves have mysterious names but none suggestive of buried gold, silver or jewels. The names, however, are romantic enough for any Treasure Island — Lady Walker's Cave, Happy Hole, Otter's Cave, Wherry Hole and Hell Hole (on the Great Saltee) and Salt Hole (on the smaller island).

Nothing is known, incidentally, of the Lady Walker who gave her name to the cave on the Great Saltee. There is a tradition that she was a noble lady who was killed by bloodhounds in the cave but this may be an imaginative story concocted to explain reddish stains on the stones within the cavern. From time to time some of these red-flecked slabs have been brought to the mainland to serve as floorstones in kitchens of local farmers.

In 1594 there occurred an event which pushed the Saltees and Ballyteigue Bay even further into prominence in correspondence of the period. In that year a Spanish privateer[7] sailed in past the Saltees and dropped anchor in Ballyteigue Bay. A party of 20 of the "pirates" came ashore near Kilmore Quay, at a place called Ilangobock,[8] made for Ballyteigue Castle about half a mile inland and carried off the owner, Richard Whitty, to their ship.

A Kilmore fisherman, Walter Devereux, who was questioned by the Spaniards, barely escaped with his life, for they told him that they would have hanged him had he been an Englishman!

Lady Walker's cave on Great Saltee, an ideal place for hiding plundered goods.

It appears that these Spaniards were not "pirates" in the accepted sense but merely privateers engaged in spying activities against England. Their ship had been sent to inquire after another vessel which had sailed from Spain for Ireland in the previous year carrying the Archbishop of Tuam, Thomas Fitzgerald, brother of the Earl of Desmond, John Lacy and others, and of which no news had since reached Spain.

The second vessel, sent to make inquiries, took Richard Whitty back to Spain so that some idea of the situation in Ireland might be got from him. He was set at liberty and allowed to return home soon afterwards. His capture and detention occasioned much correspondence in the State papers of the time, evidence of the consternation among the English authorities in Ireland at the temerity of a Spaniard privateer to enter home waters.

Nor was this the only occasion when pirates kidnapped local people. The famous petition[9] of John Boxwell, tenant of the Saltees, in 1707, mentions that his brother had been carried off by French privateers who raided the islands almost weekly, and that he was never heard of again.

This petition of 1707 affords a sidelight on the War of the Spanish Succession (1702-1713) which was fought between France on one side and the Grand Alliance of England, Holland, Austria and other states, on the opposite side.

King Louis XIV of France wanted to place his grandson, Philip of Anjou, on the Spanish Throne. The Grand Alliance opposed this expansionist plan and an eleven-year war was waged to prevent its implementation. Louis succeeded in his objective, for the Treaty of Utrecht, which ended the war, gave the Spanish crown to Philip, but also laid down that his heirs should not claim the kingship of Spain thereafter. Under other clauses in the Treaty Spain ceded Gibraltar to Britain, and France ceded Newfoundland to Britain.

During the war French privateers were apparently very active around the

John Paul Jones, who fought the British in the waters round the Saltees. (From an old engraving).

41

south-east coast of Ireland, harassing merchant ships of the enemy and, when in need of provisions or water or while sheltering from storms, regularly raided vulnerable points along the coast. The Saltees seemingly were raided almost every week, the privateers carrying off cattle for fresh meat — and once, John Boxwell's brother.

Boxwell, of Lingstown, was tenant of the islands to Major Andrew Knox, the owner of the Saltees at that time. The correspondence arising out of Boxwell's petition is given here as it was presented in the newspaper columns. The petition was eventually referred to a committee. The results are not on record:

Wexford, 20th October, 1708.

"MAY IT PLEASE YOUR HONOUR — In Obedience to your Honrs letter of the 30th of June last I have fully informed myself concerning Mr. Boxwell's Petition about the islands of Salteese and I doe find as in his Petition set forth that Boxwell is tenant to Major Andrew Knox and that he pays him the Rent of Fourteen pounds per ann. which lye between the Harbours of Wexford, Rosse and Waterford. — I know myself as well as by the account I have from the Coast Officers that the said Islands are Molested and Invested by Privateers almost every week and I doe verily believe that they doe take cattle or anything else that can be for their purpose constantly out of the said Islands and on Monday last being the eighteenth Instant John Boxwell, Nicholas Whitty and Mary Hone came before me and proved that the said Boxwell from time to time had lost or taken from him by several French Privateers since this war to the value of over fifty pounds Ster, and that one of the Privateers since this present war began carryed of one of the said Boxwell's brothers from the said Islands, and that he never heard from him since."

(Signature illegible)

To their Excies the Lords Justices and Council,
The humble peton, of John Boxwell

Humbly Sheweth — That yor petr holds the Islands of Salteses containing 250a or thereabouts situate betwixt the harbours of Wexford, Ross and Waterford by lease from Andrew Knox, Esqr Majr of the Fort of Kinsale, and that your petr pays for the sd Islands the yearly rent of £14.

That the said Islands since the beginning of this present war have frequently been molested by privateers infesting the Coasts of Waterford, Wexford, Ross, and other adjacent ports, who anchor, land and destroy your petrs Cattle grazing on the sd Islands victualling and watring their ships and furnishing themselves with other necessaries of your petrs Effects. — That the sd Islands lie contiguous to the aforsd ports are made by the sd privateers a defence against the injuries of the weather, your petnrs Cattle and other Effects being a support to them during their abode there, and her Majts Subjects and Shipping considerably prejudiced by the insults of their enemies. That the last French privateer that was brought into this Harbour by Capt. Saunders had killed and taken off the sd Island sevrl Cattle. That the Cattle taken by the sd privateers at several times amounted to the sum of £50 and upwards. That yor petr had a relation since the present warr carried off out of the sd Islands by the sd privateers and never heard off since. That yor petr is destitute of any other way to discharge the growing Rent he is by his lease lyable to pay yearly Except by stocking the sd Islands with Cattle wch tends to the advantage of her Majts Enemies discouragement of the Trade of the Inhabitants of the adjacent ports wch yor petr is likewise apprehensive will Render him obnoxious to your Excies displeasure and submitts these his difficult Circumstances to your Exceies and Lordps.

May it therefore please yor Excies and L.ps to consid. yor petrs Circumstances and to grant him such a Sume for his past losses as to yor Excies shall Seem meet, and if yor Excies and Lo.ps will agree with yor petr for the rent of the said Islande yor petr will leave the Same wast, or otherwise give directions herin as to yor Excies and Lordps in yor great wisdom shall Seem meet. And yor petr will ever pray, &c.

JOSEPH HENRY, Agent

By The Lords Justices and Council

Narcissus Armach   R. Freeman, C.

Ordered that within peton of John Boxwell be and is hereby referred to the Chiefe Comrs and Govrs of her Majts Revenue in this Kingdom to examine into the sevrl allegations thereof and forthwith report to us a true State of the whole matter. Given at the Council Chamber in Dublin the 11th day of February 1707-8.

Inchiquin, Blessington, Cha. Feilding, R. Flynne, Robt. Doyne, T. Fairfax, Cha. Dering.

To Their Excies the Lords Justices & Council

May It Please Your Excies & Lords — In obedience to yor Excies and Lordps order of Refference on the person of John Boxwell, we have examined into the sevrl allegations thereof, and on the best information we can gett, we do find and report.

That the petr Rents the Islands of Saltesses at fourteen pounds per ann, that the sd Islands have been, and are frequently infested by privateers, who take the Cattle and what Else they can find there, for their purpose. That one of the privateers carried off from the sd Island one of the petrs Brothers, who was never heard of since, and that the petr has lost at sevrl times upwards of £50 by the sd privateers, and for the reasons aforesd we are humbly of the opinion the petr may deserve your Excies and Lordps favour.

Which is humbly submitted to yor Excies and Lordps Consideration.

J. South, Sam Ogle, The Everard.

Custom House, Dublin
12th Nov. 1708.

To Their Excies the Lords Justices and Council of Ireland

The humble Petition of John Boxwell

Sheweth — That yor Petr petitioned this honble. Board in the yeare 1707. That yor Petrs said Petition was referred to the Comrs of her Majs. Revenue and a Committee of this honble. Board, who made their Reports thereon.

That in the Fire that happen'd at the late Council Chamber, the sd Petn Reports and Entries thereof were burnt, but your Petr having had the good Fortune to keep Copies of them wch are hereunto annexed, prays the same may be read.

That yor Petr being informed that the concordat hath bin ever since over drawn, discouraged your Petrs. application to this honble Board, until now obliged by his necessary affairs. And humbly prays your Excys and Lordps to consider the Premises and to grant such Order therein as to yor Excys and Lordps in yor great Wisdome and Goodness shall think fitt.

And he will ever pray, &c.,

JOHN BOXWELL

By the Lords Justices and Council of Ireland

ORDERED — That the within petition of John Boxwell and the petn &c annexed be and are hereby referred to a Comtee of the whole Board or any three of them to consider the same and fortwith to report their opinion what is proper to be done therein.

By the Lords Justices and Council

Narcissus Armach, R. Freeman, C.

Ordered — That the foregoing petition of John Boxwell and the annexed Report of the Commissioners of her Majsts. Revenue be and are hereby referred to a Comte. of the whole Board or any three of them to consider the same and forthwith report their opinion what may be fitt to be done therein.

Given at the Council Chamber in Dublin
the 22nd day of November 1708.

Will, Dublin, Abercorn, Blessington, W. Kildare, St. Geo., Clogher, Kerry, Shelburne, Robt. Doyne, Rob Rochfort, John Percivale."

The pirates who infested the seas around the Saltees were as exotic as the names of the caves on the islands. Besides the "Biskayners" (Frenchmen from the Bay of Biscay) and "Dunkirkers" (from North France), there were also North African corsairs and privateers cruising in these waters at the time. These Barbary Coast pirates or "Algerines"[10] had a reputation for ferocity and rapine that struck terror into traders, crews and authorities alike. In the years 1630-40 Viceroy Wentworth initiated a campaign to rid the coasts of the pirates but this apparently failed, as we find numerous complaints about them in the State papers of the 18th century as well.[11]

The Great Rebellion of 1641 and the years of the Catholic Confederacy of Kilkenny saw renewed naval activity around the Saltees — this time by the ships of the Confederates. Wexford was the chief port and naval base of the Confederacy and Irish frigates, based in Wexford, Fethard and Duncannon. were engaged in numerous encounters with English vessels in the waters around the Saltees. There is on record a report about one James Sutton, of Fethard. who "went out in a frigate of Captain Doran's, and other frigates that were based at Wexford, and took several English Protestant ships" near the islands. There is a further report about "Symon Synnott", who "was a pirate and went to sea in a frigate commanded by Capt. John Rossiter, by which frigate much pillaged goods were brought into Wexford, taken from the English".[12]

At the start of the Rebellion, in 1641, an English armed merchantman, the "Hopewell", out of London laden with provisions, ran ashore at Bannow. The local Confederate leader (either Cullen or Meyler by name) took Captain Rowland Langram and his crew prisoners, commandeered the cargo and guns and took the "Hopewell" out to the Saltees where they cast her away. Her guns, "five iron peces of 9 foote longe with some powder" were brought to Wexford and used on the walls there in 1649 when Oliver Cromwell attacked the town and captured it through the weakness of the commander of the castle. Captain James Stafford.[13]

Lewis, in his "Topographical Dictionary of Ireland", says that Stafford. after the capture of Wexford and the massacre of many of its citizens, retired to the Great Saltee and "built a cottage there which still bears his name".[14] Kathleen Browne, the Co. Wexford historian, in a booklet published in 1940, however, wrote that Stafford was not guilty of treachery and that he lost his life, and his family and relations their lands, in the Cromwellian war and confiscations. However the islands were still experiencing the depredations of privateers well into the 18th century. They were a favourite rendezvous for raiders of the fledgling American Navy in the Revolutionary War of 1775-1783 and the legendary John Paul Jones[15] cruised these waters and took many prizes within sight of the Saltees. As late as 1768 a member of the Boxwell family, who farmed the Great Saltee, obtained compensation from the Government for cattle of which he was plundered by American privateers who frequently anchored off the islands, probably to replenish meat and water supplies.

In Kilmore Quay and along the south Wexford coast stories are still told of the Saltee pirates and their exploits and not a few of the tales were regarded as mere tradition until a few years ago. Then, in a strange manner, at least one of the pirate stories was proven true in grim fashion.

Local fishermen for generations had retold the tale of a laden merchantman which was once pursued into Ballyteigue Bay by a privateer. The pirate ship hauled off as night fell, in the conviction that the other vessel was well and truly trapped in the dangerous bay and could be captured and boarded at ease at dawn.

But the captain of the merchantman had a trick up his sleeve. When darkness had descended he had his crew lower a raft on which was rigged a light on a short mast, then doused their own ship's riding lights. The strong tide carried the lighted raft away from the anchored merchantman towards the northern tip of the Little Saltee and, seemingly, the open sea. It was followed by the pirate ship whose captain obviously thought the merchantman was trying to get away under cover of darkness.

The raft floated on over the rocks of St. Patrick's Bridge and the pirate ship, unaware of the danger, followed. She struck a hidden rock near the tip of the Little Saltee and sank. In the darkness and confusion, the story went, many of the pirates were drowned. Others managed to get ashore on the island and there buried the less fortunate of their comrades.

Tradition in Kilmore Quay for years held that the remains of these pirates were buried there. Then, a few years ago, fishermen, including Mr. Jack Devereux of Kilmore Quay, found skeletal remains laid bare by tide and erosion. The skulls and bones were re-interred nearby by the Kilmore men. Further proof of the strange occurrence was provided by other fishermen who, when trawling in the vicinity of the place where the pirate ship was wrecked, found rusted guns and cutlasses[16] in their nets. The rock on which the vessel foundered is locally known as Privateer Rock.

Other tangible relics of this colourful era in the story of the Saltees were the four ring-bolts and cradle of the flag-pole, on the highest point of the Great Saltee, on which signals were raised to warn people on the mainland that pirates or privateers were approaching.

It seems that the islands were used by smugglers in years gone by also. So much so that it was found necessary to post two waterguards there in the 19th century.[17] "We remember brown and swarthy smugglers" wrote Mr. & Mrs. S. C. Hall in 1855[18] — and well they might, for smuggling was rife along the entire coast at the time. There are many stories told about smuggling in the Saltees area, usually involving brandy, rum and wine. According to the stories the contraband liquor was transferred to local fishing boats at sea and stored in caves along the coast, at places such as Fethard, Blackhall, Lacken and Bellary. And what better place to transfer contraband at sea than behind the Saltees!

There is a tradition in the Boxwell family that one John Boxwell of Lingstown was drowned off the Saltees while trying to recover a keg of rum which had gone adrift. An account book kept by Ambrose Boxwell of Butlerstown Castle records the importation of wine direct from France to Bargy Castle,[19] home of the Harvey family who were related to the Boxwells. Needless to remark direct importation of the wine avoided payment of duty to the Government — in short it was smuggled in.

Another story told locally concerns a man named Wisby Jeffers who lived on the Hill of Cullenstown and who came into possession of five gallons of smuggled rum. He brought it home — only to hear that the Revenue men were searching houses all along the coast. Not wishing to waste the precious liquor and yet fearful of the consequences if it were found in his possession, Wisby devised a plan. He made a huge pot of stirabout, using the rum as a mixer. The Revenue man never found those five gallons of contraband liquor — but Wisby was drunk for six full days afterwards!

On another occasion when a ship with a cargo of rum ran ashore on The Burrow, near Kilmore, local fishermen cheated the coastguards and Revenue men by wading out to the wreck, filling their long, rubber boats with rum and then, by tying them together and slinging them over their shoulders, carried the rum ashore under the very eyes of the minions of Government.

Even in much more recent times precious cargoes have changed hands behind the Saltees, with not even the ghosts of long-dead Revenue men and coastguards to throw up their spectral hands in horror.

Thus ended a colourful, if bloody, chapter in the saga of the Saltees. But before the 18th century was to close, the islands were to see another tragic episode in their long history — the capture, which led to their execution, of two of the leaders of the 1798 insurrection who had taken refuge there.

FOOTNOTES – CHAPTER 6

1.   The Saltees were "famous in the sea calendar, for to mariners the sound was, for a long period, one of fear" — Mr. & Mrs. S. C. Hall, in *Ireland, Its Scenery and Character,* Vol. II.

2.   The normal tides, flowing through the Sound, between the Great and Little Saltees, reach a rate of five or six knots. Elsewhere along this coast swifter tidal currents are encountered. A geologist examining the sea-bed off Carnsore Point, the site of a proposed nuclear power station, told me that he and his fellow-divers experienced tide-races of eight knots at times.

3.   Hore records the source of this report as being in the State Papers of Ireland, Vol. 2, 7, 10, Jan. 7th., 4 Edw. VI., Public Record Office, London.

4.   Philip Herbert Hore, *The Barony of Forth,* in *The Past,* No. 1, Nov. 1920, from his sources collected in the Public Record Office, Dublin, before their destruction.

5.   "The Irish fishermen give intelligence all along the coast to the Biskaners (pirates from the Bay of Biscay) where the King's ships are, so that they use all means to escape us" — Captain Hookes, from Waterford, July 19, 1630, to the Lords of the Admiralty. — P. H. Hore, quoting State Papers of the period, in *The Past,* No. 1, 1920.

6.   State Papers, Ireland, No. 260, P.R.O. London.

7.   At this time, fear of Spanish aid to Ireland was never far from the minds of the Dublin Castle authorities. The movements of Irish chieftains such as Hugh O'Neill were closely watched. Thus any hint of collaboration between the Spanish and Irish touched off alarms in Dublin and London. Richard Whitty lived to the fine age (for those times) of 77, dying at Ballyteigue Castle on December 8, 1623. (For further details of this strange abduction, see Michael Meyler's article, "How Whitty went to Spain", in the *Journal of the Old Wexford Society,* No. 5, 1974-75).

8.   Ilangobock, a corruption of the Irish "Oilean Gobach" i.e. "beak-like" or "jutting island". The place so named is probably the little peninsula now known as "The Forlorn" (another corruption, from "The Far Loan" i.e. "The Far Land" in Forth and Bargy dialect). There is yet another name for this small promontory — it is Crossfarnogue Point. Joyce *Irish Names of Places* says Crossfarnogue means "The Cross of the Alders" though there is also reason to believe that it may mean "The Cross of the Lookout Post", a valid descriptive title.

9.   The Boxwell petition to the Lords Justices for compensation for his losses in pirate raids, and other relevant documents, were printed in the *Wexford Independent* of August 18, 1849, having been copied (probably by the editor, Edward Hore) from the original State Papers in the Rolls Court, Dublin.

10. The sack of Baltimore, in Co. Cork, immortalised by Thomas Davis in his poem of the same title, was carried out by Algerian pirates on the night of June 20, 1631. The two Algerian vessels involved were piloted up the intricate channel by one Hackett, a Dungarvan fisherman who had been captured at sea for that purpose.

11. In 1653, the captains of the naval gunboats 'The Rector' and 'True Love' were instructed to "clear the coast from pirates who were lying off the coast of Wexford," and in 1658, one Nicholas Codd of Forth was arrested for "keeping correspondence with pirates".

12. This and the previous report were transcribed by P. H. Hore from various State papers and were published by him in *The Past*, No. 1, 1920.

13. Stafford, born at Ballymacane Castle, Co. Wexford, in 1608, was in command of Wexford's strong-point when Cromwell besieged the town in October, 1649. "The enemy entered the gates by the treachery of Captain Stafford", wrote Carte in his *Life of Ormonde*, Vol. II, p.63. Stafford has also been described as being unskilled, "a young man, vain and unadvised", Cox's *Hibernia Anglicana*, appendix XI VII.

14. Lewis published his Dictionary in 1837. I can find no local tradition about "Stafford's cottage". There is a cliff called "Stafford" on the Great Saltee but it is not known if this has any connection with Capt. James Stafford.

15. Father Joseph Ranson's *Songs of the Wexford Coast* has a sea-chanty describing an encounter between John Paul Jones in "The Black Prince" (a famous American Frigate) and a British vessel. The running battle began near the Saltees and ended with the defeat of the British man-o-war at Strangford Bar. (See chapter on "The Saltees in Verse and Song").

16. One such cutlass, in remarkably good condition, is in the fine collection of weapons in Mr. Aidan Kelly's licensed premises in Wexford town.

17. See Martin Doyle's *Notes and Gleanings relating to the County Wexford*, Dublin, 1868. The waterguards, or coastguards, were drawn from the Coastguard Station at Crossfarnogue.

18. In *Ireland – its scenery and character*, Vol. II, (Hall, Virtue & Co. London, 1855). Mrs. Hall, nee Anna Maria Fielding, was reared in Bannow and knew the area and its way of life well.

19. The present owner of Bargy Castle, Col. Charles Davison, tells me that before a sea-wall was built half a mile from the castle, the waters of the tidal Lough of Lingstown (which also lapped Lingstown Castle) used to flow a mile up the valley past Bargy Castle and into the moat (now dry) which surrounded the castle. There was a landing stage (still visible) for boats 50 yards from the "front" door. It would have been easy to smuggle boatloads of wine and brandy into the Lough of Lingstown and up the tide-way to the castle in by-gone years.

An engraving of the Great Saltee – from Hall's "Ireland".

Chapter 7
Capture of Rebel Leaders

The decisive battle of the Insurrection of 1798 in Co. Wexford was fought at Vinegar Hill, outside Enniscorthy, on June 21st of that fateful year. There, outnumbered and outgunned, the Wexford army was defeated by a superior British force under some of the Crown's most experienced generals.

On the same day, Wexford town, which had been held by the insurgents for 23 days, surrendered to Brigadier-General John Moore,[1] and several of the local rebel leaders returned to their homes in south Wexford. They were hoping that peace proposals, being carried by envoys to the British commander-in-chief in the field, General Lake, would prove acceptable and that their lives would be spared.

These local leaders included Cornelius Grogan of Johnstown Castle, Beauchamp Bagenal Harvey of Bargy Castle and Dr. John Henry Colclough of Ballyteigue Castle.

Grogan was an old man, over 70, sick and incapacitated through gout. He hobbled about on crutches, his hands covered with warm gloves even in the hot summer of 1798. He had been a most reluctant participant in the Insurrection and had, in fact, been forced into service of sorts in Wexford town because of his position as a leading Protestant gentleman in the county.

The manner in which the Grogans secured Johnstown Castle and estates[2], including the Saltees, is an interesting one. The castle and lands, comprising thousands of acres in south Wexford, had previously belonged to the Esmondes who had forfeited their estates after Cromwell's "pacification" and "re-distribution" of lands in 1656. According to one account,[3] the Cromwellian soldier "to whose lot it had fallen" was General Monck, later Duke of Albemarle, but he sold the estate in 1683 to John Grogan, a Yorkshire clothier who had settled in Wexford town.

A second account[4] gives a different version. "Johnstown," it says, "comprised portion of the landed property granted to Lt.-Colonel John Overstreet as his lot for arrears of pay, as he had served in the Cromwellian army. On his death his widow married Edward Whithers and, by patent of Charles II, the lands were granted to him and his wife in 1667. There was no issue of this marriage and, by agreement, they settled the land, after their own use, on John Reynolds of Wexford and his wife who was a niece of Benet Whithers alias Overstreet, with remainder to their daughters, Mary, Jane and Susan Reynolds. In 1682, John Grogan of Wexford town married Mary Reynolds, the eldest of the three sisters, who was entitled to one-third of the Johnstown estate. He entered into possession of his wife's portion and, subsequently, in 1692 he purchased the other two-thirds of the property from Jane and Susan Reynolds. The successors of John Grogan continued to live at Johnstown Castle and the last to reside there was the late Lady Maurice﹒ FitzGerald who came into the property as heiress of her mother who was the wife of H. K. Grogan-Morgan, one-time member of Parliament for Co. Wexford. Johnstown, after the death of Lady Maurice FitzGerald, was handed over by her next-of-kin as a gift to the State, and is now used as a model place for farming".

The discrepancies in the two accounts in respect of the ownership of the estate may be explained by the probability that General Monck sub-let his grant of lands to Lt.-Col. Overstreet. Portion of the estates was later recovered by Sir Thomas Esmonde, after a protracted lawsuit following the Restoration. But the Saltees remained part of the Grogan estate until the 20th century.[5]

During the intervening years there were various leasings and mortgagings of the islands. In the Registry of Deeds, Dublin, there is a memorial dated November 7, 1740, conveying the lease of various lands, including the Saltees, held by Charles Gore, Earl of Arran, to John Grogan of Rathmacknee. These had previously been conveyed by the Earl of Arran to Andrew Knox in 1723[6].

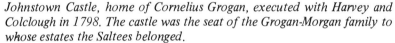

Johnstown Castle, home of Cornelius Grogan, executed with Harvey and Colclough in 1798. The castle was the seat of the Grogan-Morgan family to whose estates the Saltees belonged.

But of more immediate interest is a lease, also recorded in the Registry of Deeds, dated August 29, 1770. This lease, to which reference will be made later, throws considerable light on the Boxwell connection with the Saltees and also on Bagenal Harvey's association with the islands.

Beauchamp Bagenal Harvey was 36 in 1798, a member of the Irish Bar and a Protestant of liberal views and republican sympathies. A member of the United Irishmen from 1792 he had been arrested at the start of the Insurrection and lodged in Wexford jail. When the town was taken over by the insurgents he was freed and made Commander-in-Chief of the Wexford army, probably against his will. He was in command at the battle of Ross where his plans failed to be carried out and he was appalled at the disaster in which so many of his friends, neighbours and tenants were killed. He returned to Wexford where he headed the Town Committee and, on its surrender, retired to Bargy Castle, where his wife Judith had remained. He was apparently confident that peace terms would be agreed on and that he and his possessions would survive. To further his cause, he sent some cattle to the British military authorities in Wexford — to no avail, as it turned out.

His friend and near neighbour, John Henry Colclough of Ballyteigue, was aged 30 in 1798 and held a medical qualification. He too was a man of liberal principles but was probably opposed to physical force as a means of achieving freedom. However, he was present at several battles during the '98 campaign and his name, as a consequence, was on the Crown's list of "rebels".

Both he and Harvey soon heard disquieting reports that General Lake was not disposed towards a reasonable settlement, and together with his

Bargy Castle, home of Bagenal Harvey, the 1798 leader who was captured on the Great Saltee.

(Colclough's) wife they crossed over to the Great Saltee for temporary refuge, hoping ultimately to take ship to safety abroad.

The Great Saltee was being farmed at the time by a family named Furlong whose home was the house and tavern now known as "The Wooden House" in Kilmore Quay. The islands were well known to both Harvey and Colclough and they were familiar with all the natural features, including the caves on the bigger island.

Harvey's association with the Saltees arose through the tenancy of the islands held by his cousins, the Boxwells of Sarshill.[7] In the Registry of Deeds in the King's Inns in Dublin there is preserved a lease[8] dated August 29, 1770, under which George Grogan Knox, of Rathmacknee, leased the two Saltee islands, which had formerly been leased to John Boxwell, deceased, to Samuel Boxwell of Sarshill. The agreement was on behalf of John Grogan, who is described as assignee of the Earl of Arran, and the rights leased with the islands included "hunting, hawking and fishing". But it is the names of the lessees which are most interesting: the lease was to run "during the lives of Samuel Boxwell, John (his son), Bagenal Harvey and James Harvey, sons of Francis Harvey". The annual rent was £34.2s.6d.

Here is written evidence of Bagenal Harvey's association with the Saltees — as a young country gentleman he must have, many times, visited the islands with his cousins, the Boxwells, to shoot, fish or picnic.

The Furlongs, who farmed on the Great Saltee, were apparently the Boxwells' sub-tenants at the time. John Colclough, who lived at Ballyteigue Castle, within sight of the islands, was also familiar with them and probably visited them with the Boxwells and the Harveys. He too must have known about the cave, at the southern end of the Great Saltee, where the two leaders and Colclough's wife took refuge.

This cave, afterwards called "Colclough's Cave", was described by Thomas Cloney, another '98 leader, thus:[9] "On this island is a subterranean dwelling, the abode perhaps of an anchorite of the olden times, where these gentlemen vainly hoped to conceal themselves until they would find an opportunity of escaping to England." [10]

I doubt very much if either Harvey or Colclough, both intelligent men with unrivalled local knowledge, hoped to escape detection in the Saltee cave. All the evidence, and tradition, point to the likelihood that they intended their stay on the island to be temporary and that they hoped to escape by ship to another country.

At any rate, here the two men and Mrs. Colclough sheltered for four days and nights, aided no doubt by the friendly Furlongs. Under normal circumstances their sojourn would have been idyllic. The weather was unusually warm and dry. They had plenty of food and drink and "a feather bed" to sleep on. The Saltees at the time would have been a haven of peace in contrast with the frightful situation on the mainland where fighting continued, where hundreds were being rounded up and jailed, where executions, torture and pillage were becoming daily events in Co. Wexford. The hunt for Harvey and Colclough was intensified. The trail soon led to Kilmore.

One of the first houses visited by the searching soldiers was the home in Kilmore of the Furlong family, sub-tenants of the Great Saltee. The redcoats seized one of the Furlong boys and a family tradition holds that he was "half-hanged" from one of the big meat-hooks in the ceiling of the kitchen, in an effort to get him to inform. [11]

The fact that the soldiers seemed to concentrate on the Furlongs points to the likelihood that the information at their disposal linked the family, through their association with the Great Saltee, with the insurgent leaders. It appears that the authorities were already aware of the likely hiding-place of the two refugees.

For many years tradition in the Kilmore area had held that Harvey and Colclough were betrayed. Running through all the stories about their capture are persistent references to an informer named Waddy who seemingly knew where the leaders had taken refuge and who passed the information to the authorities.

Recent research and examination of papers in the 1798 collection in Dublin Castle confirm these stories. Harvey and Colclough were betrayed and the informant's name was Richard Waddy. [12] He is named in several documents in the State papers, including a petition[13] from a Lieutenant William Browne, of the Royal Navy, and William Wilby, commander of a revenue cutter, both of whom sought a reward for capturing Harvey and Colclough. But the most incriminating document of all is a letter from Waddy himself to the military authorities seeking "the reward offered for the apprehension of B. Bagenal Harvey".

The petition of Lieutenant Browne and William Wilby tells the story of the capture of the two leaders. Dated November 2, 1799, it is addressed to "Lord Cornwallis, Lord Lieutenant and Governor General of Ireland, and Commander-in-Chief of His Majesty's forces in that Kingdom". It runs: **"Petition of William Browne, Lieutenant in his Majesty's Royal Navy, and William Wilby, Commander of the Rutland Revenue Cruiser, on behalf of himself, his officers and crew.**

Sheweth:

That the said William Browne being employed in the Impress Service at Waterford under the command of Captain Edward Iggulden in June, 1798, volunteered to act against the rebels then in possession of the Town of Wexford, and having received Captain Iggulden's permission sailed on board the Louisa gun boat to assist his Majesty's forces in taking the Town, but it being retaken a few hours before his arrival he put himself under the command of Captain Robert Keene of the Navy, commanding officer afloat, and under his directions procured Pilots and regulated the Harbour.

That on 24th June Captain Keene directed the petitioner William Browne to proceed on board the Rutland revenue cruiser in pursuit of the Rebel Chiefs and to take on board Lieutenant Turner of the 2nd or Queen's Regiment of Foot with a party under his command, also a Mr. Waddy who informed Captain Keene that he was acquainted with all the places for concealment on the Saltee Islands, in which services Captain Keene also ordered a Boat manned and armed from his Majesty's Sloop the Chapman to assist.

That both the Petitioners immediately sailed on the said service and having landed on the Great Saltee Island made a diligent search there for six hours without success or without any other assistance from Mr. Waddy than his accompanying them, upon which the petitioner Browne proposed that the Boats should be manned and armed and rowed round the Island to search the Caves and Cliffs and that Lieutenant Turner with his party should remain on shore and answer signals from the Boats, which proposal being acceded to by Lieutenant Turner both your Petitioners went on board the Boats accompanied by Mr. Waddy.

That the Boats having rowed almost entirely round the Island, Mr. Bolton first mate of the Rutland cruiser observed some stones that appeared to have been placed by art and in consequence of this appearance the party landed and discovered the Cave in which Mr. Bagenal Harvey and Mr. Colclough were secured whom they secured and brought Prisoners to Wexford as also lodged there a Chest of Plate which the Petitioners understand is of considerable value and is now lodged in the Treasury.

That notwithstanding Mr. Waddy was not in any way instrumental to the discovery of the said Harvey and Colclough or more useful on the occasion than any private of the party he has, as your Petitioners are informed, alleged that it was he that discovered them and claimed a Reward offered by the British Government for their apprehension.

Your Petitioners therefore pray that your Excellency will be pleased to communicate this statement to the British Government in order that such share of the said reward as they may be thought entitled to be ordered to be paid to them.

Which is humbly submitted to your Excellency
Wm. Browne, Lt. R. Navy".

The petition has a commendation attached from Lt. General Johnson, stating that Browne was "an active good officer".

This version of the capture of Harvey and Colclough dispels many of the myths which had surrounded the event and confirms Waddy's role in the pursuit and capture of the two leaders. Another version [14] of the story, handed down in the Harvey family, says that Mrs. Colclough — not mentioned, strangely, in Lieutenant Browne's petition — had been washing linen in the cave and threw the soap-suds into the sea at the mouth of the cavern. These were spotted by the searching soldiers and the leaders' surrender followed.

A third version, retold by Mr. and Mrs. S. C. Hall, says a soldier saw smoke rising from a crevice in the rocks under his feet and this was found to come from a cave of considerable depth. An officer went down and called on the refugees to surrender. John Colclough then tied a white handkerchief to a stick and emerged, followed by his wife and Harvey.

Whatever the manner of their discovery, Harvey and Colclough were taken on board the cutter which sailed for Wexford.

Watching all this activity with mounting anxiety was a small group in a fishing boat lying off the island. In the boat, which belonged to a Kilmore fisherman, was a man named Denis Sinnott, of Tomhaggard. He was a follower of Bagenal Harvey. His brother Patrick had fought at the battle of Ross where he had lost an arm. Because of this wound, from which he was still recovering, Patrick had deputed his younger brother Denis to aid Harvey. The small party in the fishing boat had been lying off the Saltees, pretending to be fishing, but actually awaiting the arrival in the area of a ship which, hopefully, could be stopped and which would take Harvey and Colclough to France or America. [15] But their plans and hopes died as they watched the two leaders being taken on board the Rutland which headed eastwards for Carnsore Point and then

Left – The capture of Harvey and Colclough as depicted by George Cruikshank.

Below – Caves on the south-west shore of the Great Saltee. "Colclough's Cave" was situated further along this shore, to the left.

Wexford.

On June 27 the two men, and old Cornelius Grogan, were tried by court-martial and sentenced to death. On the following day, June 28, they were hanged on Wexford Bridge, the structure all three had helped to build only a few years previously.[16] Their heads were chopped from their bodies which were then flung into the Slaney. The heads were stuck on spikes above the door of the Courthouse which at that time faced on to the bridge.[17]

All three of their bodies were later recovered from Wexford Harbour. Harvey's remains were buried with Colclough's in the Colclough family grave in St. Patrick's churchyard in Wexford town. Grogan's body and head were interred in Rathaspeck cemetery adjoining Johnstown Castle estate.

But their spirits were not allowed to rest in peace. The vultures were soon squabbling over the spoils. The £1,000 reward offered by the British Government for the apprehension of Harvey had not yet been paid out by July 5, 1799 when Richard Waddy wrote to Lt.-Col. Littlehales of General Lake's staff.[18]

Referring to himself as "being the person who was sent by Gen. Lake to take B. B. Harvey, the Rebel General, a prisoner, on the Saltees," Waddy said "the General represented his services to his Excellency the Lord Lieutenant who was graciously pleased to consider them." Waddy goes on to say that General Lake, as a result, asked him to meet him at Dublin Castle. Unfortunately for Waddy the French landed at Killala on the day of the appointment and Lake had to rush to the west to take command of the British troops in the field. As a result Waddy did not see him in connection with the reward.

Waddy adds that he had done duty at Wexford as a yeoman during the winter and spring and had not an opportunity of meeting Lake again. He asks for Littlehales' patronage "in representing my situation to his Excellency and requesting an immediate payment of the reward offered for the apprehension of B. Bagenal Harvey". Waddy was, apparently, intent on pursuing the spirit of Harvey beyond the grave.

General Lake, in a note[19] addressed from Cork on July 12, 1799 commented on Waddy's letter. He noted that Waddy "gave the information of Harvey's having fled to the Saltees" and, with an officer's party of the Queen's Regiment, apprehended him there.

"I had offered a reward of two or three hundred guineas for him," wrote Lake, "to which they certainly are entitled, if it has not already been paid. But I have every reason to believe that the reward Mr. Waddy refers to is £1,000 offered in England for Harvey which I rather think was of (though I am by no means certain) a subsequent date to his apprehension at Wexford which both Mr. Waddy and the officer of the Queen's Regiment imagine themselves entitled to."

I can find no record of any payment to Waddy, Lieut. Browne or William Wilby. Waddy by this time had removed himself from Co. Wexford and was living at Merrion Square, Dublin. Perhaps he was fearful that these spying activities, which including informing on many others involved in the 1798 Insurrection, might be uncovered.[20] Undoubtedly his role in the capture of Harvey and Colclough was widely known in South Wexford. To this day his name is linked with those of the rebel leaders, though not with the same *turners of the Wordieens Regiment of Foot with a party under his command, also a Mr Waddy who informed Captn Keene that he was acquainted with all the places for concealment on the*

Saltee Islands, in which service Captn Keen, also ordered a Boat manned and armed from his Majesty's Sloop the

Above – A few lines from the petition of Lt. William Browne seeking a reward for the capture of Bagenal Harvey, and referring to "Mr. Waddy".

Right – Waddy's signature on his letter to Col. Littlehales requesting payment of the reward for capture of Bagenal Harvey.

fond remembrance, needless to remark.

The British Government itself was embroiled in trouble over the estates of Grogan and Harvey. The doubtful legality of their and Colclough's trials placed the Government in an embarrassing position from which they attempted to extricate themselves by passing an Act of Attainder in October, 1798. This was given retrospective force in order to legalise the executions. The same Act enabled the Government to confiscate the estates of Grogan and Harvey.

The Crown succeeded in establishing title of Grogan's estate (including presumably, the Saltees) and it was granted to Grogan's brother, John Knox Grogan.

Harvey's estate, however, presented a more difficult problem. After his arrest on May 26 and while in jail in Wexford, Harvey had executed a deed of settlement of his estates, antedated to August 1, 1797, in the hope of rendering them not liable for forfeiture.

He was not successful in this, however, and his estates were declared forfeit and leased back to his brother James who returned from his studies of agriculture in England to take up residence in Bargy Castle.

In 1810 James petitioned for a grant of the estates and a patent was issued to him on September 22 of that year. It appears that Harvey's widow, Judith, continued to reside at Bargy Castle for some time after the rebellion.

Eventually the estates were restored to Harvey's other brother John, who died unmarried and left them to his first cousin John, the eldest son of John Harvey of Tagunnan.[21]

John Colclough's widow and baby daughter, Colclough's only child, inherited Ballyteigue Castle and lands.[22] She afterwards married a Captain Young and both lived in the castle until their deaths. Their only daughter sold the place to a Mr. Edward Meadows, from whom it passed to Mr. Thomas Grant whose family are still in possession. The present head of the family is Mr. Robert Grant.

After 1798 the Saltees themselves entered a more peaceful era. But the seas around them were to see much drama and many drownings in the 19th century — a century of ship-wrecks that gave the adjacent sea-area the grim title of "Graveyard of a Thousand Ships".

FOOTNOTES – CHAPTER 7

1. Brigadier-General (later Sir) John Moore, one of the more humane of the British officers engaged in the '98 campaign. He had fought as a captain/lieutenant in America, in the Mediterranean area in the war against France, in the West Indies and, after the 1798 campaign, in Egypt, in the Baltic and in Spain. At the battle of Corunna (Jan. 16, 1809) he was fatally wounded. The poem "The Burial of Sir John Moore" by Rev. Charles Wolfe, commemorates his interment in the battlements of Corunna.

2. It seems that, at some time between the middle of the 16th century when the Colclough estate included the Saltees, and the middle of the 17th century, when we find the Saltees attached to the Grogan estate, parts of the Tintern Abbey lands changed hands. As these originally were Church lands, they may have been appropriated in the Cromwellian "settlement" and given to General Monck. In this way the Saltees could have become attached to the Grogan estate, remaining so until this century and the implementation of various land Acts in the early 1900s.

There is another possible explanation of the change of title — through marriage. Vesey Colclough of Tintern, a member of Parliament, and High Sheriff of Wexford in 1767, married Katherine, daughter of John Grogan of Johnstown in August 1765. Was there a marriage settlement which gave some Tintern lands, including the Saltees, to Grogan at that time? Or did such a transfer take place earlier, when a Colclough (Anthony, of Rathlin, Co. Wexford), married Mary, daughter of William Esmonde of Johnstown in 1634? Esmonde was MP for Wexford and a Confederate, while Anthony Colclough, although a Protestant, was a member of the Supreme Council of the Kilkenny Federation in 1642. Both suffered the loss of their estates afterwards.

3. *Chronicles of the County Wexford* by George Griffiths.

4. "Jottings of the Past", *The People,* Wexford, July-August, 1949.

5. An inquisition on the lands of Cornelius Grogan of Johnstown Castle, dated July 13, 1799, included the Saltee Islands — Quit Rent Office Collection, 1798 Papers, Public Record Office, Dublin. A further return (in the same collection) of the rental of lands forfeited by Grogan after 1798 included the Great Saltee, the tenant of which was Samuel Boxwell and the tenure "four lives from 1772". The annual rent was £34.2s.6d.

6. The Earls of Arran (family name Gore) also bore the title "Baron Saunders of Deeps", Co. Wexford. Sir Arthur Gore, first Earl of Arran, married Jane, daughter of Richard Saunders, of Saunderscourt, Co. Wexford, on March 16, 1730. Apart from this connection with County Wexford, there is a link between the Gore and Knox families which might explain the Earl of Arran's memorial referring, inter alia, to the Saltees.

This link originated in the marriage, on March 25, 1761, of Francis Knox, of Rappa Castle, Co. Mayo and Mary, daughter of Paul Annesley Gore, brother of the first Earl of Arran. Their son, James Knox — Gore, incidentally, was MP for Taghmon, Co. Wexford, in the last Irish Parliament. (Burke's *Landed Gentry* and *Irish Family Records*).

7. There was considerable inter-marriage between all south Wexford families, not least the landed Protestant gentry. The links between the Harvey and Boxwell families, for instance, were numerous. John Boxwell of Lingstown Castle (referred to in the petitions in the previous chapter) married his first cousin, Elizabeth Harvey, daughter of Ambrose Harvey of Bargy Castle in 1700. Their son, also John Boxwell, born in 1701, married another Elizabeth Harvey, a daughter of Rev. William Harvey of Bargy and also his (John's) first cousin. Bagenal Harvey's mother was another Harvey (Martha), daughter of Rev. James Harvey, of Killiane Castle, Co. Wexford — Burke's *Irish Family Records*, 1976.

8. Lease, recorded in Registry of Deeds, King's Inns, Dublin: Book 294, page 649, No.196051.

9. Cloney's *Personal Narrative of 1798*, published in 1832. "Colclough's Cave" no longer exists. Situated then beneath the low cliffs south of the Ring on the Great Saltee, it has since been eaten away by the sea. The site was pointed out by older fishermen from Kilmore Quay in the early years of this century. Cloney, incidentally, is the only chronicler of the period who says that Mrs. Colclough took her young daughter with her to the Great Saltee.

10. Harvey, according to one record, took a considerable amount of personal belongings with him to the Great Saltee. Charles Jackson's *Narrative* (1798) says Harvey took with him "a feather bed, a keg of whiskey, a tub of water, a live sheep, a crock of pickled pork, a chest of the family plate and other comforts". The chest of family plate suggests the hope of refuge abroad where the plate could be sold to provide interim finance.

11. A tradition handed down in the Furlong family. "The Wooden House" was later owned by the Suttons. It is so-called because part of the licensed premises is formed of the deck-house of a wrecked ship. Another local tradition says that when the British soldiers were searching the Kilmore area, they entered a public-house on the Millroad, near Kilmore village. The tavern was owned by Paul Colfer. The soldiers drank the place dry, promising to pay on their return. But they never paid a penny.

12. Several local sources in south Wexford, together with at least one written account, identify Waddy as Dr. Richard Waddy, of Clogh East Castle, in the Barony of Forth. He is said to have been Chief Coastguard officer for the area and therein, say the traditions, lay the cause of his personal vendetta against Harvey in particular. The suspected involvement of the Harvey family in smuggling is said to have given rise to this enmity. How tragically ironic it would be if this "pastime" of the young country squires had led to their eventual betrayal and death! Waddy was a descendant of a Captain Richard Waddy, a Cromwellian soldier who was granted Clogh East Castle in 1654. This had been the property of James Codd who was killed at the siege of Duncannon in 1645. Captain Waddy married Codd's daughter and with her received all the deeds and papers of the original owner. The last Waddy to reside at Clogh East Castle was Dr. John Waddy who died without issue on January 15, 1875. (See "Jottings of the Past", *The People*, Wexford, August 5, 1949).

13. Lieut. Browne's petition for reward, 620/56/114, State Papers Office, Dublin Castle.

14. This version of the capture was given in 1938 by Bagenal Harvey's grand-nephew, the late Very Rev. Canon Harvey Bradish, Rector of Clonegal, Ferns. (In collection of the Folklore Commission, University College, Belfield, Dublin).

15. The information about Denis and Patrick Sinnott was handed down in their family. Patrick's daughter, Dolly Sinnott, married Thomas Doyle of Lingstown. Their daughter, Catherine, married a John Cardiff who emigrated to Uruguay where he was killed. His and Catherine's daughter, Sarah, married John Carty whose daughter, Mrs. Katherine Ryan, M.A., Dublin Road, Skerries, Co. Dublin, gave the story to the author. Mrs. Ryan's mother, Sarah Carty, had heard the story directly from her grandmother, Dolly Sinnott.

16. Grogan, Harvey and Colclough, with numerous other landed proprietors and business-men in Co. Wexford, had formed a shareholding company which financed the building of Wexford Bridge in 1795. The present bridge is built almost on its site.

17. Sir Jonah Barrington, a personal friend of Harvey, and the author of *Personal Sketches of his own times* (1827-32), saw the severed heads of Harvey and Colclough over the Courthouse door: "The heads....... appeared black lumps, the features being utterly undistinguishable".
    The executioner was a sergeant of the King's County militia, of the name of Dunn.

18. In Rebellion papers, State Papers Office, Dublin Castle, 620/58/115.

19. As above.

20. Waddy also informed on Thomas Dixon and his wife Margery of Wexford; John Murphy, of Loughnageer; Morgan Byrne of Castlesow; John Howlin, formerly captain of an American privateer "who committed several acts of piracy off the coast of Wexford"; and Edward Roche, of Garry-lough — Letter dated August 15, 1798, to Dublin Castle, S.P.O., 620/39/175.

21. The information about the estates of Grogan and Harvey is derived from the Quit Rent Office Collection of 1798, in the Public Record Office, Dublin, and summarised in the 59th Report of the Deputy Keeper of Public Records. Additional information from Burke's *Irish Family Records*. The latter work, incidentally, errs in saying that Harvey died unmarried. His wife was the former Judith Steevens of Arklow whom he married in 1797 — See *The Wexford Rising in 1798* by Charles Dickson, p.191.

22. The first Colclough mentioned in possession of Ballyteigue Castle is Thomas Francis Colclough, son of a John Colclough, in the early years of the 18th century. He was probably John Henry Colclough's grandfather.

Chapter 8
Graveyard of
a Thousand Ships

Between Hook Head to the west and Tuskar Rock to the east at the entrance to the Irish Sea, the rocky, indented coastline of south Wexford, with its numerous jagged crags, hidden reefs and treacherous shoals, presents the most dangerous coast in Ireland for shipping. Added to those hazards are the lack of sheltered bays or harbours and the ferocity of the tidal currents in the area. Here is a rock-bound coast fully exposed to the prevailing southerly and south-westerly winds. Here the tides race in east-west directions — so strongly that their currents move like great rivers, spilling over St. Patrick's Bridge, swirling round the islands and the numerous rocks and reefs in this dreaded sea-area.

Here is "the graveyard of a thousand ships", its entrance marked on the landward side by Hook lighthouse, its southerly limits extending to the Coningbeg lightship, guardian of the Coningbeg and Coningmore Rocks south of the Great Saltee. Once inside these dreaded outposts, in the days of sail, a ship driven by a southerly or south-westerly gale had little chance of survival.

A study of the map shows that Ballyteigue Bay is like a huge trap — its jaws corresponding to the Hook Peninsula on one side and, on the other, the line of rocks, reefs and islands extending from the mainland at Kilmore and including St. Patrick's Bridge, the Saltees themselves, the Brandies and the Coningmore and Coningbeg Rocks. Within the arms of this trap lie further hazards — Baginbun Head, the Keeragh Islands and the deceptively attractive Burrow of Ballyteigue, its seven miles of curving beach and sand-dunes luring the unwary with a prospect of safe landfall.[1]

Beyond the Saltees, to the east, are more dangers — Black Rock, Tercheen, the Barrels (marked by a light-buoy) and the granite fist of Carnsore Point, ready at all times to pound an errant ship to pieces. Only when Tuskar Rock is rounded and the Irish Sea opens up ahead can the mariner feel safe.

This truly was a coast of fear for generations of seafarers. It earned its grim title in the days of sail. Even today ships steer clear of this "graveyard" and its two sinister tombstones, the Saltees.

I have described the sea-approaches to this area as if sailing in from the west or south-west — for this is the route taken by thousands of homeward-bound vessels leaving the Atlantic and making through St. George's Channel or up the Irish Sea to the great trading-ports of Bristol, Cardiff, Liverpool, Manchester, Dublin and Wexford itself. After the natural hazards of the dangerous coastline the second reason for the vast number of ships wrecked here was the fact that the main trade-routes to some of the busiest ports in Britain and Ireland passed close by.

But there was a third reason for the numerous shipwrecks on this coast. In the 18th century, many vessels, after making the long Atlantic crossing, invariably ran close to Hook lighthouse which often was their first landfall. Through errors of navigation or judgment, or because of fog and storm, the masters often mistook the Hook light for that of the Eddystone, off the coast of Cornwall. As a result they steered right into Ballyteigue Bay, believing they were running up Plymouth Sound. The unfortunate captains usually discovered their mistakes too late. In one year alone, 1803, no fewer than 11 large sailing ships were wrecked between the Hook and Kilmore, most of them victims of this navigational error.

In his *Statistical Survey of the County Wexford*[2] (1807), Robert Fraser discusses this subject and a possible remedy: "Ballyteigue Bay," he writes, "presents a wide opening mouth of 15 miles from Hook light to the Saltees and is extremely dangerous...... It is but a few years back, when the Captain of a West-India packet mistook the tower of Hook light for the Eddystone lighthouse off Plymouth Sound, and in running as he thought for Plymouth, was brought up by the coast of Wexford. A similar mistake happened lately by a homeward-bound West Indiaman, and a cargo of the value of £120,000 was with difficulty saved by some fishermen."

An old engraving of the ancient tower on Hook Head which is Europe's oldest lighthouse.

As a remedy against such disastrous errors Fraser advocated the setting-up of a system of lights on the Saltees which, by their positioning, would warn all ships when they were getting too close to the dangers of Ballyteigue Bay.[3] For various reasons, however, this plan was not put into effect. For one thing, a lighthouse or set of lights on the Saltees would have to be positioned on the highest point of the islands (Big Head, Great Saltee, 198 feet high) to have the desired best results. But, on this site, the light or lights would be in danger of being obscured by fog or low clouds by reason of its height above sea-level.

Instead of Fraser's plan, a lighthouse was built instead on Tuskar Rock and was first lit in 1815.[4] This beacon, together with those of the Coningbeg lightship[5] and the Barrels[6] buoy, help vessels to steer clear of Ballyteigue Bay and its dangers.

Even so, the number of wrecks in the Bay since the erection of Tuskar light seems to imply that there might still be a case for a light on the Saltees.

Samuel Lewis also noted the dangers of the Bay when he wrote his *Topographical Dictionary of Ireland* in 1837: "The Coningmore Rock, always above water, lies a mile and a half (S. by W.) from its (Great Saltee) south-west point and about a mile (S.W. by W.) from it is the Coningbeg Rock, which appears at half-ebb. Outside of these rocks is placed a light ship, having two lanterns at an elevation of 25 feet above the sea at high water mark, displaying a bright light visible at a distance of nine nautical miles in clear weather. From the islands (Saltees) to Hook Tower, a distance of five leagues the intermediate space is a large bay with a continual in-draught and a heavy sea setting in towards the shore, and dangerous from rocks and shallows,

Jagged rocks at the eastern end of the Great Saltee, and the tidal waters of the Sound, were but two of the hazards facing ships in this area. In the background is the Little Saltee.

known only to persons well acquainted with the coast. Numerous vessels have been wrecked here; should a vessel get too far into this bay, it is impossible to beat out, and there is no place of refuge, except Fethard, which though it has a small pier, can afford no shelter from the shallowness of its waters, and its exposed situation".

Numerous other commentators, travellers and seafarers have, down the years, recorded the dangers of this sea-area. Navigation manuals to this day warn the mariner of its treacherous features.

In their time Samuel Carte Hall and his wife Anna Maria had personal experience of sea disasters here: "Our memory can recall many cases of frightful shipwrecks off the Saltees, the Keeroes, Burrow of Ballyteigue and what — by right of affection — we call our own Bannow".

Records of early wrecks are scarce. One noteworthy disaster occurred in 1645 when the flagship of the English fleet, engaged to assist and protect Duncannon during the siege of the fort in that year, went down in a storm off the Tower of Hook, and the Admiral and all his crew perished. A recent suggestion that this wreck might be worthy of the attention of divers was probably made without reference to the fact that little or nothing would be left of the hull by now, owing to the force of the tides in the area which could tear a ship to pieces in a very short time.

Divers and salvage teams investigating wrecks off the coast of south Wexford have found that no wooden ships survived on the seabed there, and that even iron hulls were shattered after a time. The wreckage of a French trawler which struck the Little Saltee in 1972 bears awesome testimony to the power of the seas here. In less than two years the iron hull was smashed into twisted, unrecognisable bits of wreckage which now lie rusting among the rocks on the southern shore of the Little Saltee.

Those eleven large vessels which were wrecked in 1803 between the Hook and Kilmore would not have survived very long. Griffiths, in his *Chronicles* refers to these wrecks: "The winter of 1803, following a remarkably warm and dry summer, was unprecedented for the severeity of its storms. There were eleven large vessels wrecked between Kilmore and the Hook lighthouse, and many more must have foundered off the coast, from the quantity of masts, spars, and dead bodies that were driven ashore."

Fraser, writing in 1806, mentions that during the previous winter "no fewer than seventeen ships of large burthen are known to have come ashore on Ballyteigue Strand." This spate of disasters was exceeded in 1861, incidentally, when on one day, February 7, seven ships were wrecked on the entire Co. Wexford coastline.

Out of the great number of shipwrecks on or in the vicinity of the Saltees, it is possible to describe only a few. A fuller, more detailed list of wrecks appears as an appendix to this chapter.

Probably the most celebrated shipwreck, though not by any means the most disastrous, in the area occurred at the beginning of the 19th century. The ship involved was a schooner, "The Foxwell", bound for Wexford with a cargo of cotton bales and casks of wine. Caught in a fierce gale one winter's night, the schooner struck a rock near the Saltees and broke in two. Her crew managed to scramble on to the rock where they huddled throughout the night. When daylight came the captain consoled his men, thanking God that they were all safe so far. "Not all, captain," replied one of the crew. "Long Philip has gone down with the ship." "Long Philip," the nickname of the missing hand, was known to be fond of drink. "May the Lord have mercy on him," remarked the captain. "He must have been in the spirit store when the ship struck."

All that day the gale drove giant waves against the rock on which the sailors huddled. Among them were two boys who clung to a Newfoundland dog, the ship's mascot, for warmth. Wet, cold and hungry the crew had to endure another twenty-four hours on the exposed rock. During the second night some of the men urged the captain to kill the Newfoundland dog and divide the flesh among them, so afflicted were they by hunger. The captain was about to sacrifice the dog when several boats appeared on the now-calm, moonlit sea. They quickly rescued the shipwrecked crew and took them to safety in Kilmore.

Not until then did they know that their rescue had been brought about by the man they believed had been drowned, "Long Philip". Apparently, as the captain had rightly suspected, Philip had been in the spirit store when the ship struck and split in two. The crewman had either been drunk or unaware of the extent of the disaster, and stayed in the hold. The bales of cotton kept his half of the wreck afloat and it drifted ashore on the Burrow. Here "Long Philip" was found in a comatose condition, two days after the ship had foundered.

He quickly recovered and, when questioned, was able to tell the local people about "The Foxwell" and the course she had been taking. The Kilmore fishermen rightly agreed that, if there were survivors, they would be on the Saltees or nearby rocks, and headed their boats immediately in that direction. They were just in time to rescue the captain, crew and Newfoundland dog, all of whom received the best of hospitality and help from the Kilmore people. Next day they were taken to Wexford, accompanied by "Long Philip", now restored in status in the eyes of both captain and crew.

Despite their ordeal, the crew of "The Foxwell" were more fortunate than those on board the emigrant ship "Glasgow" which was wrecked on the Barrels Rocks on February 15, 1838.

The Barrels are two rocks lying close together about three-quarters of a mile, east-south-east, from Black Rock. They are visible only at low water and for many years had a lightship stationed some distance outside them. The ship was later removed and a light-buoy substituted. There was neither ship nor buoy to warn the "Glasgow" on that stormy day in 1838. On board were ninety-five emigrants, most of whom were from the West of Ireland, and seventeen crew-members. The ship had left Liverpool on February 8, bound for New York.

After being detained in St. George's Channel by adverse winds and hazy weather until the 14th, the "Glasgow's" captain, William Robinson, found himself in sight of Tuskar light. The night became hazy and at 5 a.m. on the 15th, while running at nine knots, the "Glasgow" struck the Barrels.

The violence of the impact swung her round and the stern struck the rocks, unshipping the rudder. Having all sails set she struck a third time and was swept over the rocks into deep water. But she had been holed and the sea rushed into the passengers' quarters below. Terrified, the emigrants rushed on deck and there huddled, cold, wet, and afraid to return below. In this state they were discovered by the little "Alicia" of Wexford, bound from Dublin to Newport, under Captain Martin Walsh.

Hearing the bell of the "Glasgow" tolling in distress, skipper Walsh bore up towards the sound and tried to run the "Alicia" under the "Glasgow's" lee quarter. The crew of the "Glasgow" could not use their boats as the oars had been swept away, so Walsh ordered them to let a boat with a crew drift towards the "Alicia" and provided them with oars. With lines out to both ships this small boat then took off most of the women and children in small numbers while Walsh stood by in the "Alicia".

The storm began to worsen and Walsh saw that the "Glasgow" was now sinking swiftly. At great risk he ran his own schooner alongside the "Glasgow". The ships collided twice, carrying away the "Alicia's" bulwarks and channels, and tearing her mainsail. Striking a third time, the flukes of the "Glasgow's" anchor went through the bows of the "Alicia". But the brave Walsh, himself at the helm, sailed round the "Glasgow" until he had succeeded in getting eighty-two people on board. He was making a final run when he saw the "Glasgow" lurch and disappear beneath the waves. Of those who had been left aboard, Captain Walsh managed to rescue four more from the sea. The other twenty-six were never seen again. The "Alicia" remained in the area for some time, then sailed for Wexford which was reached the same evening.

The survivors were succoured by the townspeople and eventually sent to their homes in the west. Captain Walsh and his crew were feted and honoured in every port to which they later sailed, especially in Glasgow, the home-port of the wrecked ship's captain and crew. Captain Walsh was guest of honour at a civic banquet, when a valuable testimonial was presented to him by the city's merchants and bankers.

A few years later, the "Alicia" was returning from the Black Sea with a cargo of corn. Captain Walsh put into Falmouth for orders and was windbound for some days. When the weather changed he set out again for Wexford. That night a violent storm arose and the "Alicia", her gallant captain and crew were never heard of again.

In Kilmore the saga of the wreck of the "John A. Harvie" is still recounted, even though it occurred almost one hundred years ago, on November 24, 1880. The "John A. Harvie", a three-masted barque of Windsor, Nova Scotia, was carrying a cargo of maize from New York when she was driven aground at the White Hole, Tacumshane, a few miles north east of the Saltees.

There was no life-boat in Kilmore at the time[7] and when the alarm was raised the nearest life-boat, based at Carne, twelve miles away, had to be pulled on a massive trolley by a team of horses by road to Kilmore.

So fierce was the storm, however, that the Carne crew refused to put out in their boat, which was propelled by sails and oars. By this time, the "John A. Harvie" was beginning to break up. Two of her masts has snapped and had to be cut away by the crew who were then forced into the rigging of the remaining mast. Even there they were in danger of being swept away by the gale-force wind and mountainous seas. Their plight was being watched in mounting horror by the coast inhabitants.

Among the onlookers on the shore were two local priests, one of whom,

Father O'Gorman, called for volunteers to man the Carne life-boat. The fishermen who stepped forward included John Monaghan, Johnny Madden, John Radford, Tom Dillon, John Walsh, Larry Clarke, and Luke Rochford. Paddy **Kavanagh**, the cox of the Carne lifeboat, also volunteered.

There was a late addition to the crew when Tommy Clarke was shamed into going by Father O'Gorman. Tommy, who was a bad attender at Mass, was nevertheless known to the priest as a skilled boatman. He may have been reluctant on this occasion to risk his unshriven soul. So Father O'Gorman had to bully him into going on the lifeboat. "Come on, me man," said the priest, "you've only one life to lose." So, as the story goes, Tommy went.

The Carne life-boat was launched, the priests wading into the waves to bless the craft and its crew. After a titanic struggle out to the "John A. Harvie", the life-boat took off the barque's crew and brought them safely ashore.

After that rescue, the story concludes, the life-boat was taken from Carne and based in Kilmore.[8] Another, and kinder, version of the saga says that when the life-boat reached the stricken barque, the crew refused to leave the rigging, so bad was the storm. Next day the Carne men manned their own life-boat and took them off.[9]

Down the years numerous wrecks have occurred on the Saltees themselves and in their immediate vicinity. Several rocks in the area bear the names of the ships which were wrecked on them. The incident which gave Privateer Rock its name has already been recounted. Water Witch Rock, east of St. Patrick's Bridge, is so-called after the steam-boat of that name which was wrecked there in a terrible storm in 1833. Several lives were lost when she went down. At the western end of the Little Saltee there is a rock called the "Fairy Queen", named after a ship which struck it and sank sometime in the closing years of the 19th century. It is said that this vessel was carrying a cargo of muskets for South Africa when she was wrecked.

The year 1837 was a particularly disastrous one for shipping in the area. On January 24 the "Shanaccadie", bound for Liverpool with a cargo of cotton from Brazil, was wrecked at Kilmore. The crew were saved through the efforts of the local people. [10] On February 5 the brig "Maria" was wrecked at Ballyteigue. Next day, two vessels, the "Mary" and the "Betsy", both bound for Dublin, were wrecked at Kilmore. The crews were saved. A French brig, with a cargo of wine, was lost at Ballyteigue on December 2, 1843.

On January 30, 1850, the brig "Fairfax" of Jersey, bound from Sierra Leone for Liverpool with 470 tons of palm-oil, was wrecked at Ballyteigue. Again the crew were saved by local people. On February 1 of the same year the "Horatio" of Sunderland, bound for Dublin with a cargo of wheat from Alexandria, was wrecked at Kilmore. The crew were saved. In the following year, on January 16, the "Grace", bound from Alexandria for Preston, was wrecked on St. Patrick's Bridge. The captain, Henry O'Neill, and one seaman were lost.

On January 18, 1854, the "James Calder", sailing from New Orleans to Liverpool with 2,000 bales of cotton, was wrecked in Ballyteigue Bay. The crew were saved "by the exertions of the inhabitants of the district and the coastguard".

Two years later, in 1856, the "Isabella" was wrecked on the rocks off

Kilmore. Her crew of five were rescued by the coastguard. On March 11, 1868, the "La Touche", a French ship, was wrecked in Ballyteigue Bay and her entire crew perished.

The rusted remains of an iron sailing-ship are still to be seen at the Haven, between Kilmore harbour and St. Patrick's Bridge. The ship was "The Wayfarer", sailing in ballast, and she was wrecked here in 1871. Flints from her ballast are still found in the vicinity.

On Feb. 20, 1874, the "Glide" of Waterford was lost off Ballygrangans; her crew were saved. A tug, the "Brother Jonathan", was wrecked off the Saltees on Feb. 30, 1879.[11] The "Liffey", of St. John's Newfoundland, with a cargo of deal, went aground near Kilmore on Nov. 2, 1881, and, after a fierce battle with the raging seas, her crew were brought safely ashore.

On July 4 of the same year, the 3,152-ton White Star Liner "Brittanic" ran aground in fog off Kilmore Pier. En route from New York to Liverpool, the liner had called at Cobh but ran into thick fog. For two days she steamed at snail's pace along the south coast of Ireland, completely lost. She eventually struck ground off Kilmore Pier but was not badly damaged. The two hundred saloon passengers and some steerage passengers were taken off by the ship's boats, landed at Kilmore and transported to Wexford on horses' and asses' carts. The "Brittanic" was refloated at high tide but took with her a huge chunk of rock wedged in her bottom. Off Wexford Harbour this rock dropped out and water started to rush in. The liner called for assistance and was towed to Rosslare Harbour where temporary repairs were carried out. She sailed a couple of days later for Liverpool.

The wreck of the Turkish ship "Mermeriss",
which foundered on Tuskar Rock on June
29, 1895.

The close of the 19th century saw more wrecks in the area. On Christmas Day, 1895, the brigantine "Citizen of Youghal", laden with coal, was wrecked on the south-west tip of the Little Saltee. Two of her crew, the captain and a seaman, were lost; four others were saved. On April 7, 1898, the barque "Haweswater" of Liverpool, in ballast, was wrecked inside the Saltees.

In the memory of one man living into the 1930s, there were thirteen wrecks on The Burrow at one time at the end of the 19th century. He recalled the names of two, the "Atle" and the "Enterprise". Another of the wrecked ships had carried a cargo of rum and sugar — it was probably from this wreck that local people smuggled rum ashore in their rubber boots.[12]

From yet another of the wrecks a steam siren was salvaged and attached to a threshing engine. In the autumn, when the threshing set made its rounds from haggard to haggard, the mournful sound of the ship's siren summoned the "meitheal" to work, raising ghostly echoes over the south Wexford country-side. Wrecks are still being found in the seas around the Saltees. In May, 1976, at Kilmore Quay trawler, the "Guiding Star", found an iron hull on the bottom near the Coningmore Rock. The wreck is believed to be that of the "Idaho", an American vessel which sank after striking the Coningmore in dense fog in 1872 while sailing from Liverpool to New York.

There is an unknown wreck lying in seventy feet of water at the base of East Brandie Rock. It is completely broken up but its cast-iron propellor and steel shaft denote a steamship. Two anchors, each about six feet long, are lying nearby. North of the Brandies divers have found the wrecks of two iron ships, one lying on top of the other, while further out, south of the Great Saltee, four wrecks lie close together on the bottom. One of these has been dated

A model of Dunboyne, one of the last of the Irish full-rigged ships

about 1847, but what ships they were no one knows.

Through all those 19th century wrecks there persists a pattern — sailing ships driven into Ballyteigue Bay by south-westerly storms, finding no escape once within the confines of the bay, and ending up aground on The Burrow or stuck on the rocks of the Saltees, St. Patrick's Bridge or The Forlorn. In most cases, after the establishment of the lifeboat station in Kilmore in 1884, the crews were saved. That there were some casualties is a pointer to the ferocity of the storms and the dangers of the coast rather than to any lapses on the part of the various crews who have bravely and efficiently manned the Kilmore lifeboats down the years. Their record is a truly honourable one.

The wrecks continued in the 20th century. On November 28, 1908, a French barquentine, the "Goacuetta", carrying general cargo, was wrecked on St. Patrick's Bridge.

During the 1914-18 war numberless ships were lost in this area. The name of one of them, at least, lives on in local memory. She was the "Mary Grace", a two-masted schooner which was bombed off the Coningbeg lightship. The crew got away and were taken on board the lightship until help arrived. The damaged schooner drifted ashore at Ringbawn strand. But of wartime losses more later.

There are still people living in south Wexford who remember the wreck of the S.S. "Lennox" on the Collough Rocks, south of the Great Saltee, on January 18, 1917. Mention the "Lennox" and you'll probably get the puzzling comment: "Ah yes, that's where all the Chinese watches came from." When this 6,500 ton steamship struck the Colloughs, her crew of forty-five were saved by the Kilmore lifeboat and brought ashore to the village. Among the survivors were thirty-four Chinamen who apparently sold their watches in the local pubs and shops so that they could buy food, drink and clothing. I have been assured that some of those Chinese watches are still going strongly in the Kilmore area.

Another wreck which is vividly remembered is that of the "Valdura", which ran aground on The Forlorn on January 12, 1926. She was carrying a cargo of 4,500 tons of maize which was jettisoned in an effort to refloat her. Farmers from miles around drove carts to Kilmore and took away loads of the "yalla male", as it was called, for use as animal feed.

In the following year, on April 27, the Milford steam-drifter "Cluny" was wrecked on St. Patrick's Bridge. Her crew of eight at first refused to leave their vessel but the weather got worse and eventually, on May 2, they were taken off by the Kilmore life-boat. The "Cluny" broke up later and her boiler was washed ashore at the Haven. Another wreck occurred on the Blue Rocks, east of St. Patrick's Bridge, on September 28, 1928 when the "Brackeley", an Arklow schooner, went down. Her crew of four were saved by the local life-boat.

The 1939-45 war brought a fresh toll to the Saltee sea-area. On December 19, 1940, the Irish Lights relief vessel "Isolda", under Captain A. A. Bestic, was bombed by a German plane and sank in fifteen minutes off the Great Saltee. Six of her crew were killed by bombs; the seventeen others were rescued by the Kilmore life-boat. On October 20, 1941, another ship was bombed in the same area; her fate is not known. A month later, on November 24, the

Great Western Railway's "Rockabill" was attacked by a plane but survived. On December 22 of the same year a plane was shot down off the Saltees — the nationality and fate of its crew are unknown. On June 21, 1942, the S.S. "Lanahrone" of Limerick, carrying coal from Barry Dock to Lisbon, went aground on the Great Saltee at the Ring but was later towed off.

South of the Saltees, also, while on her last, ignominious voyage to the breaker's yard, the former fisheries protection vessel "Muirchu" sprang a leak and sank on May 8, 1947. Previously named "Helga" she had won notoriety as the British gunboat which shelled Liberty Hall during the 1916 Rising in Dublin. Afterwards taken over by the Free State Government she had served for many years as a fisheries protection vessel until she outlived her usefulness. [13] She was on her way from Cork to the Hammond Lane Foundry Co. in Dublin when she sank, eight miles south of the Coningbeg lightship. Her crew of ten and three passengers were taken off by a Welsh fishing trawler.

Both world wars (1914-18 and 1939-45) saw numerous shipping casualties in the seas south of the Saltees. In the 1914-18 war this was a favourite hunting ground of German U-boats which, on occasion, ventured into the Irish Sea and attacked shipping there. From this period date most of the wrecks which now litter the sea-bed in "the graveyard of a thousand ships".

A newspaper report in April, 1956, said marine experts estimated that there must be more than one hundred ships sunk in the area, more than half of them the victims of German submarines in the 1914-18 war. One salvage ship also discovered four U-boats lying in 25-30 fathoms of water about seven miles from Carnsore Point.

In the first year of salvage operations in the 1950s about £10,000 worth of metal was lifted from a wreck lying in thirty-five fathoms of water, five miles south-west of the Coningbeg. The salvage ships, operating from Liverpool, Southampton and Milfordhaven, retrieved undisclosed quantities of lead, copper and other valuable metals and it was believed that a wreck with gold bullion was found near Tuskar Rock.

During the 1939-45 war more ships went to the bottom in "the graveyard", the victims not only of submarines but also of the great minefield which stretched across St. George's Channel from the Saltees to the coast of Devon. [14] There are numerous stories about German submarines surfacing south of the islands to recharge their batteries and refresh their crews; of fishermen exchanging some of their newly-caught lobsters for German brandy and wine; of mysterious boats and winking lights. No one will ever know the full story of those strange happenings.

Small wonder, in view of the vast number of ships lost in the area, that superstition and imagination often conjured up ghostly vessels sweeping past in the gloom and strange lights riding where no ships can pass.

So accustomed were local people to these sights that only casual attention was paid to them. One story has it that a ghost ship was regularly seen driving under full sail over Mageen Reef where no big ship can go. On one occasion when the wraith was seen some locals were playing cards. They went to the door, took a casual look and immediately returned to their card-game. "It's the lad again," one of them merely commented.

The appearance of a ghost tugboat off the north-west coast of the Little

Saltee usually heralded a storm.[15]   A tug had once been lost in this area and people often reported seeing her there afterwards. One man who saw her reported it to the coastguard in the hope of getting the £1 reward for spotting a ship in trouble. The coastguard turned out, with all their life-saving apparatus but there was no ship there at all.

Yet another ghostly craft, according to tradition, could be seen and heard "between day and dark" returning to the landing-place at the Ring on the Great Saltee. This happened regularly, it was said, after a shipwreck at the back of the island when some workmen launched a cot from the Ring and tried to rescue people from the wreck. But the cot and its crew never returned. Frequently afterwards, according to the story, the boat was seen returning to its mooring-place and the sound of the oars grinding in the rowlocks could be clearly heard.

The S.S. Lanahrone which ran aground on the Great Saltee on 21 June 1942.

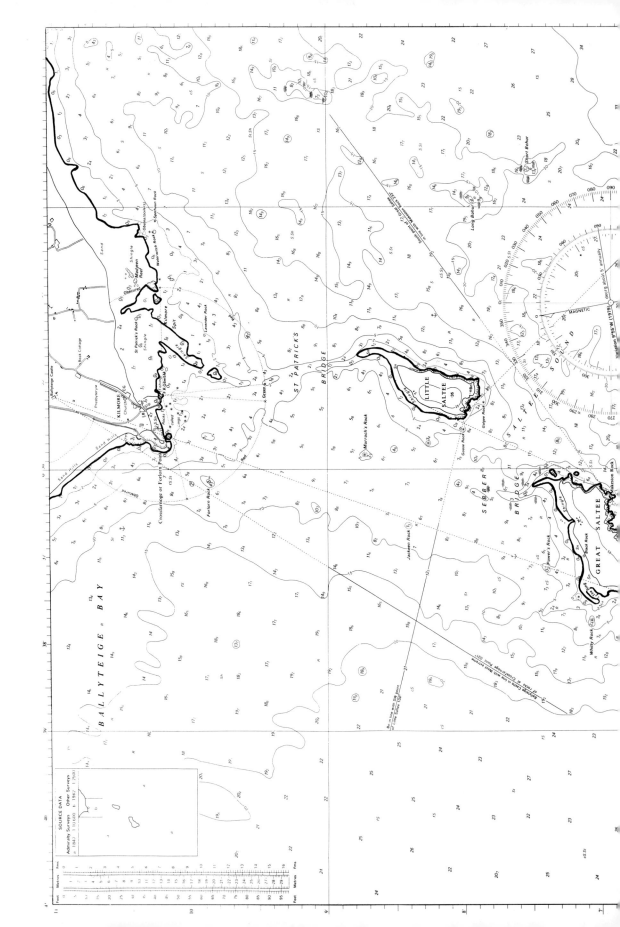

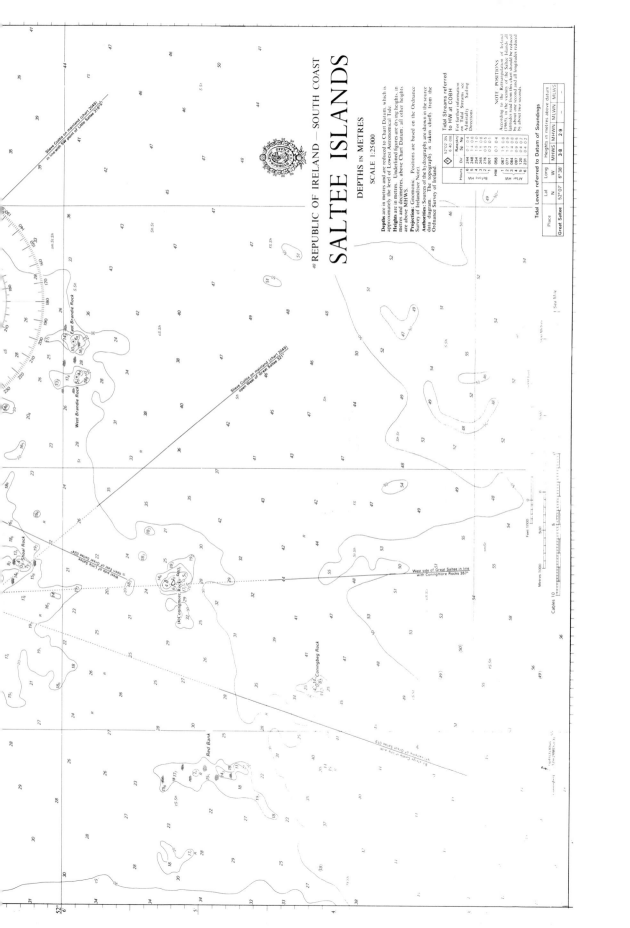

REPUBLIC OF IRELAND – SOUTH COAST

SALTEE ISLANDS

DEPTHS IN METRES

SCALE 1:25 000

Depths are in metres and are reduced to Chart Datum, which is
approximately the level of Lowest Astronomical Tide.
Heights are in metres. Underlined figures are drying heights, in
metres and decimetres, above Chart Datum; all other heights
are above MHWS.
Projection: Gnomonic. Positions are based on the Ordnance
Survey of Ireland(see Note)
Authorities: Sources of the hydrography are shown in the source
data diagram. The topography is taken chiefly from the
Ordnance Survey of Ireland.

NOTE POSITIONS
According to the Retriangulation of Ireland
(1965) in the vicinity of the Saltee Islands, all
latitudes read from this chart should be reduced
by about one second and all longitudes reduced
by about two seconds.

Tidal Streams referred
to HW at COBH

◇	52°02.3N			
	6 40.0N			
Hours	Dir	Rate(kn)		
		Sp	Np	
Before HW	6	244	0.4	0.4
	5	248	1.4	0.8
	4	254	1.6	1.0
	3	265	1.6	0.8
	2	276	0.9	0.5
	1	300	0.2	0.1
HW	058	0.7	0.4	
After HW	1	067	1.5	0.8
	2	071	1.7	0.9
	3	084	1.4	0.8
	4	097	0.9	0.5
	5	120	0.4	0.2
	6	231	0.4	0.2

For further information
on Tidal Streams see
Admiralty Sailing
Directions

Tidal Levels referred to Datum of Soundings

Place	Lat	Long	Heights in metres above datum			
	N	W	MHWS	MHWN	MLWN	MLWS
Great Saltee	52°07'	6°38'	3.8	2.9	–	–

1.   Griffiths, in his *Chronicles of Co. Wexford* refers to "that dangerous bay embraced by the Saltees and the point of Hook Promontory" and adds that the promise of safety in this bay is most delusive, "as the wreck of many a noble vessel yearly testifies".

2.   "Statistical Survey of the County Wexford, drawn up for the consideration and by order of Dublin Society", by Robert Fraser, Dublin (1807).

3.   Waterford Chamber of Commerce, backed by merchants and traders had demanded that a light should be built on the Great Saltee before a lighthouse on Tuskar was considered.

4.   The construction of a lighthouse on Tuskar Rock presented considerable difficulties, not the least of which was the frequency with which high seas swept right over the rock. On the night of October 18-19, 1812, a violent storm carried away the wooden huts of the workmen engaged in building the lighthouse on Tuskar and fourteen of the twenty-four men were drowned. The remaining ten clung to the rock until they were taken off two days later. The Tuskar light was first lit on June 4, 1815.

5.   The Coney Rocks (the original name of the Coningmore and Coningbeg) were first marked by a lightship, the "Seagull", which was established on September 1, 1824. This was the second lightship to be established off the Irish coast, the first being on the Kish Bank in 1810.

6.   The Barrels lightvessel was established in October, 1880 after a ship had mistaken the Coningbeg's two fixed white lights for the Tuskar's revolving two white flashes and one red flash, the red being not visible over 10 miles. The Barrels lightship was withdrawn in 1941 during the 1939-45 war and a lighted whistle-buoy placed in its stead. The light-vessel was re-established on March 1, 1960 and was finally withdrawn on February 25, 1970, being replaced again by a lighted whistle-buoy.

7.   A life-boat was first stationed in Kilmore in 1847. In 1850 the boat was reported to be efficient but two years later she was in need of repair and orders were given that she be taken to Wexford. There is no record of any services by this boat, and, although the name of Kilmore appears in the reports of the late 1850s as a life boat station, it appears to have lapsed for some years. It is reported in the Life-Boat Institution's journal for November 1, 1884, that the attention of the Committee of Management of the Institution had been called to the desirability of having a station at Kilmore and that a life-boat had been sent there in March of that year. She was a thirty-four foot, ten-oared, self-righting boat named "John Robert".

It may well have been the episode at the wreck of the "John A. Harvie" that prompted the provision of the life-boat at Kilmore.

8.   The Carne life-boat station, established in 1859, was not closed, in fact, until 1897.

9.   The story of the wreck of the "John A. Harvie" was related by a member of the Kilmore crew who manned the life-boat that day – John Walsh. He told the story to a collector for the Folklore Commission and it is preserved in the archives of the Commission at University College, Belfield, Dublin.

10.   Some of the bales of cotton from the "Shanaccadie's" cargo were salvaged by local people but members of the crew set the bales on fire – a strange way of repaying the debt of their rescue.

11.   The captain of the "Brother Jonathan", Thomas Griffiths, who lost his life in the wreck, is buried in Grange cemetery where his tombstone still stands.

12.   This may have been the wreck of the "Clementina" of Demerara. She was carrying a cargo of rum and sugar for Greenock and ran ashore at Ballyteigue on February 22, 1883.

13.   The "Helga" had been launched in Dublin in 1908. One of the passengers on board when she listed and sank in May, 1947, was a director of the Hammond Lane Foundry Co., the firm which had bought her as scrap. Another on board was the journalist Brian Inglis.

14.   Grim reminders of this minefield still bob to the surface in the fishing grounds off the Saltees to this day. As recently as Feb. 3, 1977, a huge barnacle-encrusted mine, weighing almost a ton, was picked up in the net of the Kilmore Quay trawler "Francesite". The mine was brought into Kilmore where an Army Officer defused it. The Channel minefield stretched from the Saltees and Tuskar to Hartland Point in Devon to keep German submarines out of the Irish Sea. During and after the war years, many mines were washed up on the shores of south Wexford – once, with fatal results, at Cullenstown when several soldiers were killed.

Previous page – The British Admiralty Chart for the Saltee Islands.

List of Shipwrecks

This list of ships wrecked on the south coast of Wexford, between Hook Head and Tuskar Rock, and on the islands and rocks off that coastline, does not purport to be complete. There are traditions and folk memories of dozens of other wrecks in the same sea area but relevant details have been lost. Neither does the list take into account the numerous ships lost in St. George's Channel in the wars of 1914-18 and 1939-45. In one small area alone, south of Tuskar, lie three large freighters sunk in the 1914-18 war. The list does not include, either, many fishing boats from south Wexford ports lost or sunk in storms such as that in October, 1898, when most of the fishing boats at Kilmore Quay were wrecked at their moorings.

Date and place where wreck occurred	Ship's name, description, nationality or home-port etc.	Lives Lost	Lives Saved	Cargo
1549, Jan. 10 South coast Wexford	----- Limerick	---	---	Wine
1645, Jan. 26 Hook Head	British flagship	Crew	---	---
1815, Feb. 21 Carnsore	*Will*, sloop Weymouth	----	Crew	---
1819 Keeraghs	*Demarara*	13	---	Gold
183? Saltees	*Foxwell*	---	Crew	Cotton Wine
1837, Feb. 5 Ballyteigue Bay	*Maria*	---	---	---
1837, Feb. 6 Kilmore	*Mary*	---	Crew	---
1837, Feb. 14 Barrels	*Glasgow* Emigrant ship, Glasgow	39	82	---
1837 Kilmore	*Shanaccadie* Liverpool	---	Crew	Cotton
1838, Nov. 25 Tuskar	*Ariadne*	6	8	Timber
1843, Dec. 2 Ballyteigue Bay	French brig	---	---	Wine
1844, Mar. 8 Carnsore Point	*Georgia* Palermo	---	---	---
1847, Jan. Keeraghs	*Niobe* New York	Crew	---	Corn
1850, Jan. 30 Ballyteigue Bay	*Fairfax* Jersey, brig	---	Crew	Palm Oil
1850, Feb. 1 Kilmore	*Horatio* Sunderland	----	Crew	Wheat
1851, Jan. 16 St. Patrick's Bridge	*Grace* Preston	2	---	----

Date / Place	Ship / Route			Cargo
1852, Jan. Hook Head	*Columbia* New Orleans to Liverpool	11	19	Cotton, Corn
1852, Jan. 8 Nr. Hook Head	*Caroline* New Orleans to Liverpool, barque	―――	―――	Corn
1852, Jan. 11 Ballyhealy	*Regalia* Jersey	―――	Crew	Barley
1852, Feb. 27 Bannow Bay	*Szarpy* Austria	―――	Crew	Flour
1852, Nov. 17 Bar o' Lough	*Grandholme* Aberdeen	―――	―――	―――
1852, Dec. 5 Tuskar	*Landgrigg Hall* Liverpool	23	2	Salt
1852, Dec. 29 St. Patrick's Bridge	Greek ship	10	―――	Indian corn
1854, Jan. 18 Ballyteigue Bay	*James Calder* New Orleans to Liverpool	―――	Crew	Cotton
1855, Jan. 11 Carne	*Hollyock* Boston	―――	―――	―――
1856 Kilmore	*Isabella* brig	―――	5	―――
1856 Kilmore	*Exile* New Ross, brigantine	―――	6	―――
1858, Jan.21 Rosslare	*Elerslie* Liverpool	―――	―――	―――
1861, Jan. Carnsore	*Brandiwine* American	―――	―――	―――
1861, Feb. 10 Tuskar	*Grace Evans*	―――	―――	―――
1861, Feb. 10 Carnsore	*Guyana*	―――	19	―――
1865, Jan. 29 Hook Head	*Panope* brig	―――	―――	―――
1865, Jan. 30 Tuskar	*Stirlingshire* barque	6	―――	Rum, Sugar
1866, Feb. 2 Carnsore Point	*Carrie Dairs* barque	―――	―――	―――
1867 Tacumshane	*Spanish Packet* brig	―――	7	―――
1868, Mar. 11 Ballyteigue Bay	French ship	―――	―――	―――
1868 Ballyteigue Bay	*La Touche* (may be same as above)	Crew	―――	―――
1869, Mar. 20 Bannow Bay	*Porteus* Cardiff brig	―――	―――	Coal
1871 Off Kilmore	*Wayfarer*	―――	―――	Ballast
1872, Mar. 26 Carnsore	*Jane and Sarah* schooner	―――	―――	Fertiliser

Date and place where wreck occurred	Ship's name, description nationality or home-port etc.	Lives Lost	Lives Saved	Cargo
1872, May 17 Tuskar	*Tripoli* Cunard Line	---	---	---
1872 Coningmore Rock	*Idaho* American	---	---	---
1873, Jan. 13 Baginbun	*Polyxna*	---	---	---
1874, Jan. 4 Tuskar	*River Krishna*	---	---	---
1874, Jan. 19 Bannow Bay	*Vittorisso G* Italy, brig	---	Crew	---
1874, Feb. 20 Off Kilmore	*Glide* Waterford	---	Crew	---
1876 Carne	*Chevereux* French barque	---	Crew	Timber
1879, Feb. 20 Saltees	*Brother Jonathan* Tug	---	Crew	---
1880, Nov. 22 Bar o' Lough	*Balla* Jersey	---	Crew	Salted Fish
1880, Nov. 24 Off Tacumshane	*John A. Harvie* Nova Scotia, barque	---	Crew	Maize
1881, Nov. 3 Nr. Kilmore	*Liffey* St. John's	---	Crew	Deal
1882, Sept. 25 Off Tacumshane	*Paquite de Terranova* Spain	---	Crew	---
1883, Feb. 22 Ballyteigue Bay	*Clementina* Demerara	---	Crew	Rum, Sugar
1883, Dec. 24 Nr. Tuskar	*White Star* Liverpool	---	---	Jute, Coal
1884, Feb. Carne	*Sem* Sabronella	Crew	---	Coal
1880's Ballyteigue Bay	*Atle*	---	---	---
1880's Ballyteigue Bay	*Enterprise*	---	---	Slates
1880's Ballymadder	*King Arthur*	---	1	---
1895, June 29 Tuskar	*Mermeriss* Turkey	---	Crew	---
1895, Dec. 25 Little Saltee	*Citizen of Youghal*	2	4	---
1898, April 7 Saltees	*Haweswater* Liverpool	---	---	---
1900, May 26 Off Saltees	*Louisa* Dartmouth	---	---	Coal
1908, Nov. 28 St. Patrick's Bridge	*Goacuetta* France	---	---	General
1914, Feb. 20 Keeraghs	*Mexico* Norway	1	10	Timber

Date/Place	Ship/Origin	Casualties	No.	Cargo
1917, Jan. 18 Gt. Saltee	*Lennox* Leith	---	45	General
1921 Splaugh Rock	*Faithful* Arklow	---	---	---
1926, Jan. 12 The Forlorn	*Valdura*	---	---	Maize
1927, May 2 Off Kilmore	*Cluney* Milford drifter	---	8	---
1928, Sept. 28 Nr. St. Patrick's Bridge	*Brackeley* Arklow schooner	---	4	---
1929, Oct. 20 Carne	*Mount Blarey* Plymouth schooner	---	5	---
1940, Dec. 19 Nr. Saltees	*Isolda* Irish Lights, Dublin	6 killed by bombs	17	---
1942, June 21 Gt. Saltee (towed off)	*Lanahrone* Limerick	---	---	Coal
1957, Dec. 19 Ballyteigue Bay	*Auguste Maurice* French trawler	---	10	---

After an American 700-ton ship, the "Antelope" was wrecked on the Saltees in 1885, her timbers were salvaged and from them a new 129-ton schooner, also named "Antelope", was built at Wexford Dockyard in 1890. This new "Antelope" was originally a two-masted schooner and was stated to be the first and only small schooner to cross the Atlantic from Wexford to St. John's in Newfoundland and bring home a cargo of timber. She was chartered on that occasion by Messrs. Jasper Walsh and Co., timber merchants, Wexford, and skippered by Capt. Clancy. Converted in 1923 to a three-masted schooner, with pole masts and an auxiliary engine, she plied the cross-Channel routes until laid up in 1930. She lay idle in the river at Arklow until 1940 when ships were again badly needed. She was then refitted with a new engine but her mizzen mast was once more removed. She ended her days after running aground on Dollymount Strand, Dublin, in December, 1950. Lloyd's tried in vain to refloat her and finally sold her for £15 to Mr. P. E. Blake, Red Cow Garage, Clondalkin, who dismantled her and blew up the hull for its valuable timber. Her broken ribs still protrude from the sand at Dollymount, a pathetic link with the glorious days of sail and with the Saltee Islands.

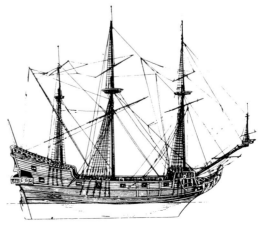

An Irish Confederate ship.

Chapter 9
19th Century Island Life

The 19th century brought to the Saltees their heyday of habitation and use for farming. Under a sub-tenancy from the Boxwell[1] family the Furlongs had farmed the Great Saltee for some years before 1800. They were succeeded by the Parles about the beginning of the 19th century. Bassett, in his *Guide and Directory*, retells a legend about the first Parles who settled in south Wexford: "According to tradition the originator of the Parle family was one of three brothers who were wrecked at Carnsore Point. Having had a leg broken he was left behind and his two brothers returned home to France. Permanent settlement in the barony of Bargy was induced by the fair native who nursed him through his illness and whom he married."

It has been suggested that the three Parle brothers may have been privateers, but exactly when they were shipwrecked on the south Wexford coast is not known. A census[2] of Co. Wexford for the year 1659 shows that there were nineteen Parles (rendered Pearle) in Bargy at that time.

By 1841 there were eight people living on the Great Saltee; fourteen by 1851, and seventeen by 1861, although these seventeen included nine men "who had charge of the light-ship lying off the Great Saltee," obviously the Coningbeg.[3] In 1871 there were only five people (three men and two women) on the Great Saltee — all members of the Parle family. At the same time there were five people living on the Little Saltee.

The population of both islands varied according to the farming seasons, with greater numbers of farm labourers living there in the Spring and at harvest-times. Samuel Lewis, writing about 1837,[4] says that "about twenty persons constitute the population," which was made up of the members of the Parle family and labourers.

Down through all the years of the 19th century we find that remarkable family of Parle in occupation of the islands. Lewis, whose 1837 work was based on the 1831 Census, said the Great Saltee was owned at that time by Hamilton Knox Grogan Morgan of Johnstown Castle,[5] and notes that of its 130 arable acres about one third was under tillage and the remainder in pasture, and "from the abundance of seaweed found on its shores, it was rendered particularly fertile."

A valuation report of 1853[6] gave the Great Saltee as being occupied by John Parle, the lessor being Susan Boxwell, and the Little Saltee occupied by Ellen Parle, with Hamilton Knox Grogan Morgan as the lessor. Both these islands were reported as having houses, offices and land. In later records[7] we find the successive heads of the Parle family listed as occupiers of the two islands, with the names of the lessors also: 1855 — Great Saltee, John Parle; lessors William and Susan Boxwell; Little Saltee, Ellen Parle; lessors, the Hon. Mrs. Elizabeth Deane Grogan Morgan, and the Countess of Granard. 1860 — Great Saltee, John Parle; Little Saltee, Francis Parle. 1864 — Great Saltee, John Parle; Little Saltee, Francis Parle. 1883 — Patrick Parle and Francis Parle.

It will be noted that some new names have cropped up as the lessors of the Little Saltee. These are the Hon. Mrs. Elizabeth Deane Grogan Morgan, and the Countess of Granard, formerly Jane Grogan Morgan.[8] Both were daughters of Hamilton Knox Grogan Morgan. Elizabeth was mother of Lord Muskerry (family name FitzMaurice), while Jane married the seventh Earl of Granard (family name Hastings Forbes).

From the latter union there were two daughters — Lady Adelaide Jane Frances, who married, on April 13, 1880, Lord Maurice FitzGerald, second son of the Duke of Leinster; and Lady Sophia Maria Elizabeth, who married, in 1885, Sir Henry C. Grattan Bellew, third baronet. His name also crops up later as lease-holder of the Little Saltee. Truly it could be said that they were keeping it in the family.

There are other names in the records, either as grantors or grantees. In the late 1880s William B. Nunn is recorded as being grantor of the two Saltee islands. In 1903, Sir John G. Barton is mentioned as grantee of the Great Saltee. In 1905, Benjamin A. W. Lett and another are given as grantors of the two islands, with William Nunn listed as grantee. As late as 1924, with Sir Henry C. Grattan Bellew and others listed as grantors of the Little Saltee, Thomas F. Crozier and another are given as the grantees.

The Hon. Mrs. Elizabeth Deane-Morgan (seated), daughter of Hamilton Knox Grogan-Morgan of Johnstown Castle, owner of the Saltees. The other lady is Miss Gonne-Bell, a relative of Mrs. Deane-Morgan.

Lady Adelaide, more popularly known as Lady Maurice FitzGerald, survived her husband (who died in 1901) by many years, and was the last of the family to live in Johnstown Castle. She presided over the dissolution of much of the estate in Co. Wexford and elsewhere which followed the passing of the 1903 Land Act. Also called the Wyndham Act, after George Wyndham, the English landlord who introduced it in the Westminster Parliament, it enabled tenants to buy out their holdings. "Under the Act, the landlord kept only the land which he actually occupied in 1903: and as this was a time of farming slump, this, on the whole, was not much: just the park or round the house, outlying woods, mountains, moors, perhaps a few village and town rents." (Burke's *Landed Gentry of Ireland,* 1958 edition).

In the last decades of the 19th century there were various transactions involving the leasehold of the Saltees: by this time the great estates were breaking up; it was a period of farming recession, and non-profit-making islands such as the Saltees were not greatly sought after. Even the hard-working Parles were finding it difficult to make ends meet. So we find Patrick Parle, in 1897, having to mortgage part of his leasehold interest in the Great Saltee to Catherine Kearns, of Commercial Quay, Wexford, and later, in 1904, selling

The old farmhouse (background) and ruins of farm buildings on the Great Saltee. The Cordylines (palms) were planted in more recent times. Since this photograph was taken, some years ago, bracken and briars have covered most of these ruins.

the remainder of his interest to Martin Pierce.

Whatever about the lease, the Great Saltee still belonged to the Grogan-Morgan estate and in 1898 we find the trustees of the estate to be Lord Maurice FitzGerald, Lady Adelaide FitzGerald, and Lord Walter FitzGerald, of Johnstown Castle.

Life on the islands in the 19th century was spartan — but apparently satisfying. Intensive tillage produced such crops as barley, wheat, oats, beans, mangolds, potatoes, turnips, and cabbage. There was ample grazing for cattle and sheep. Cows were kept to produce milk. Pigs were bred for sale and as a source of fresh pork. Hens, ducks and geese provided eggs and meat. There was an abundant supply of rabbits, and several fresh water wells which rarely went dry. Bean-stalks and timber washed up by the tides were used for firing. Seaweed was a free fertiliser.

"Crops grow well in fine seasons" Bassett noted in 1885,[9] "but in stormy weather, in consequence of having no beach at the back, the water strikes the cliffs and goes over upon the crops."

Winter storms, in fact, provided the single climatic factor disadvantageous to near self-sufficiency and continued habitation. Bad weather often cut off communication with the mainland for weeks at a time. It interrupted the regular service by island cot to Kilmore Quay, taking farm produce to market, ferrying over extra workers in season, maintaining essential supplies of paraffin oil (for lamps), coal (for the fires) and things like matches and salt. There was also the ever-present danger of accident or illness occurring during a stormy period.[10]

In the end, however, it was none of these things which brought occupation of the Saltees to an end. Ultimately it was a combination of general economic circumstances and local spiritual considerations which forced the island families to quit. Farming entered a depressed period at the beginning of the 20th century and the Parles and Whites (last tenants of the Little Saltee), excellent farmers though they were,[11] found it no longer paid them to work the islands.

Allied to this economic factor was another, less tangible, one. Local Catholic clergymen had, for many years, been concerned about the spiritual welfare of the islands' inhabitants, cut off as they often were from the sacraments, Sunday Mass, and the ministrations of the local priests. This concern was frequently transmitted to the heads of the island families. They had to pay heed to their pastors. For more than one hundred years, however, the islanders lived a full if frugal life. After the winter gales, the seaweed was collected from the rocky shingly shores and carted to the fields. Ploughing was done with the aid of horses and, at times, teams of three asses. The early crops of potatoes, cabbage and beans escaped the frost which often beset the mainland, for here the surrounding sea kept the climate mild and frost-free.

Animals were transported to and from the Saltees in the island cot, a large, wide-beamed, shallow-draught rowing boat fitted with a single sail. Straw was strewn aft in the cot which, on the mainland, was drawn up on the strand. Planks were laid from the gunwale to the sand. The animals to be transported were lassoed, thrown on their sides and had their legs tied together. Whether they were cattle, horses, sheep, or pigs, the animals were then pulled and pushed up the planks and into the boat. The ropes on their legs were tied to the rings in the cot to present lunging about. Loading or unloading out at the islands was a much more difficult task as there were no smooth beaches or landing places where a boat could be pulled up. The only near-suitable spot was at The Ring but this could be used only at certain stages of the tide. Otherwise animals had to be loaded into the cot from the water or from a smaller boat which could get in to the landing places.

Strangely, sheep were the most troublesome animals to transport by sea, and their small trotters were in constant danger of going through the bottom of the boats. One of the most docile and willing animals was a mare which was brought to and from the islands so often that she almost asked to be put aboard the cot for a trip. One day her keeper, Peter Parle of Ballyhealy, drove her to the strand for a load of woar or seaweed. A cot similar to the island craft was drawn up on the beach. The mare headed straight for it and lay down beside it, waiting to be pulled on board. She seemed most disappointed when roused to pull a cartload of woar home.

The story of White's bull is another example of the strange effect which the sea has on some animals. The bull was roped, tied up, and loaded on board a cot which was to take him from the Little Saltee to the mainland. However, no sooner was he in the cot than he broke loose and stood up — to the consternation of the boatmen. For several minutes the bull and the men eyed each other in silence, all of them, apparently, afraid to move. Then one of the boatmen very quietly told the others to start rowing. Gingerly they began to pull, trying desperately not to rock the boat. The bull stood still, legs stiff, head up, ears forward. In this manner they crossed the two and a half miles of choppy sea to Kilmore. As soon as the cot ran up on the beach, the men leapt ashore. The bull followed quietly. No one ever knew whether the men or the animal were most frightened on that memorable trip.

If that bull had plunged overboard he probably would have swum ashore — like the Kerry bullock which had been left alone on the Great Saltee. Gazing across the half-mile Sound, between the islands, the bullock could see seven cows on the Little Saltee and decided he would like some company. Next day he was found, grazing placidly with the cows, on the smaller island. Astounded locals could only assume that the bullock, motivated by some strange instinctive knowledge, chose the right time at ebb to swim across the tidal Sound. As a reward, the Whites bought him and allowed him to stay with the cows on the Little Saltee.

The farm dwellings and buildings on both islands were extensive and well-built of stone. Bassett (1885) described the Parle homestead on the Great Saltee as "a comfortable slated house, occupying a well-sheltered spot on the north-east side." This house still stands and part of it is used by bird-watchers and visitors for cooking and sleeping purposes. Round about it are traces of the farmyard — the ruined walls of outbuildings, circular stone stack-stands, a stone water-trough, a soggy duck pond — all overgrown by bracken and briars now. Here there is also the ruin of a stone building called "the schoolhouse" where, it is said, island children got a rudimentary education. On the Little Saltee there are also extensive ruins of farm buildings, roofless, lichened and silent.

The father figure of this farming dynasty on the Saltees was John Parle who lived on the bigger island until his death at the age of 87. He left a widow, a

Right — Martin Pierce, holder of the lease of the Great Saltee, who died following a boating accident off the island in 1907.

Below — Stone piers of an old gateway, appropriately called "the heavenly gate", frame a vista of wild beauty on the Great Saltee.

few years his junior, who survived him two years. One of their sons, Stephen, lost his life when he fell from the top of Celbooly cliff on the south-west end of the Great Saltee. He was only thirteen at the time. His body was recovered from the sea by island boatmen at "Deadman's Shoal", so named after this tragic discovery. [12]

John Parle was, reputedly, a powerful man. He could lift two fully-grown sheep, one under each arm, into a cot, and was known to have carried two 20-stone sacks of meal in the same manner. He and his brother Patrick kept a hospitable house on the Great Saltee. Picnic and boating parties, bird watchers or ordinary visitors who chanced to be weather-bound on the island were fed and sheltered. Fresh straw was often spread in the barn where storm-bound trippers could sleep. [13]

The late Dr. George Hadden told of a camping trip to the Great Saltee when he and his companions underestimated their appetite. Mrs. Parle baked them a huge "cart wheel" of a griddle-cake — the biggest cake of bread he had ever seen. The Whites of Neamestown, who later farmed the Little Saltee, have also been described as "a great charitable family" and "a happy people". There are many fond memories of them and of the Parles among the residents of Kilmore, many of whose parents and relatives worked and lived on the islands. [14] There was always "an egg in the gruts [15] and a rabbit in the pot" for worker and visitor alike. On fast days and Fridays only eggs were eaten — often as many as thirty eggs being boiled for the mid-day meal. Servant girls were employed to do the housework, cooking and caring for the fowl. One of these, with the strange name of "Katty the Lute" is still remembered in Kilmore. Wages were low — labourers earning 1s. 6d. (one shilling and sixpence) a week plus their board and lodging; boys who brought the cows for milking, fed the hens and gathered bean stalks for firing, got fourpence a week and their bed and meals.

For all its Spartan simplicity and frugality, life on the Saltees was, apparently, attractive enough to draw many to the islands to live and work. Folk memories dwell on the more pleasant aspects — the beauty and peacefulness of the islands themselves; the close bonds of friendship and neighbourliness between all who lived there; the camaraderie and sheer joy of living that banished loneliness and feelings of isolation. [16] True, there were hard times — when storms prevented communication with the mainland for weeks at a time; when fuel supplies ran low or when crops were beaten to the ground by summer gales; when illness struck or when death called. Yet the theme which runs like a golden thread through all the memories and stories is that life was good, if tough, and that people were kind and truly Christian.

Those were the good years on the Saltees — but good times do not last for ever. The 20th century brought many changes. The last of the Parles to occupy the Great Saltee, Patrick, gave up farming on the island in 1905 when we find a new registered occupier — Martin Pierce. [17]

After the death of Francis Parle, of the Little Saltee, Robert White farmed but did not live on the smaller island. He died in 1898. His sons William and Richard, continued the practice and in 1905 the Little Saltee was transferred from the Parles to William White. It is said that Mrs. Mary Parle of Clongaddy sold her interest in the island to William White for £150 at that time.

It was during these early years of the 20th century, with the implementation of various new land laws, notably the Wyndham Act of 1903, that the Great Saltee again became "independent". Up to this a part of the Grogan-Morgan estate, the island was purchased by John Pierce in May, 1910, and for the first time in centuries became detached from its parent estate on the mainland. John Pierce had taken over the lease of the island after the death of his brother Martin in 1907. Although he purchased the Great Saltee in 1910, his title was not registered until 1922.[18] The Pierce family used the island chiefly for recreational and sporting activities. At that time there was a small fresh-water lake in a hollow near the centre of the island,[19] and wild duck flocked there in season. Shooting parties found plentiful targets among these and among the rabbits.

The island remained in Pierce hands until 1930, when Susan Pierce of Park House, Wexford, widow of John Pierce, sold the Great Saltee for £5. The story of the sale has it that the purchaser was a waiter. In fact the island was bought by a Nicholas Brennan, of 17 Hardwicke Street, Dublin, who is described in the instrument of sale [20] as a "club steward". Mystery surrounds the identity of Brennan. Hardwicke Street, at the time, was a street of tenement houses. In the Kilmore area there persists a story that he died, penniless in a Poor House, without friends or relatives. From this story derives another which has it that a beggarman bought the Great Saltee at the time.

My own belief is that Brennan may have been the nominee of a number of sportsmen who were members of a club in Dublin. He became the nominal leaseholder of the Great Saltee which was used by the club members for shooting and fishing. During his tenure the Land Commission annuity on the island was revised, and reduced from the £39.7s.6d. of John Pierce's tenure to £25.16s.10d. a year. Claude Francis purchased the lease in July 1939 but the Land Commission advance of £1,125 given to aid the purchase of the lease was not repaid or redeemed and the annuity of £25.16s.10d. is, in fact, still alive.

Claude Dermot LeBert Francis, of Rathjarney, Killinick, Co. Wexford, who was the next occupant of the Great Saltee, seemingly foresaw a boom in farm produce prices during the war which was then imminent and immediately started to farm the island. He erected a small bungalow as a residence — it still stands — and specialised in crops of early potatoes, oats and barley. He rated the soil on the island "the best he had ever set foot on," and the four years he and his wife spent there "the happiest years of his life".

Once again during his occupancy the old fields rang anew with the talk and laughter of men and women, chiefly from Neamestown, as they gathered the early potatoes or harvested the corn. A tractor and mill were ferried out to the island to thresh the corn,[21] and according to some of the men who worked there, the threshing lasted a week. The workers lived in the old farmhouse at such times, wooden bunks being built for sleeping purposes.

Claude Francis was forced to leave the island when his wife became ill in 1943. He himself died in May, 1976 — the last person to have lived on the Saltees. He sold the Great Saltee to Michael Neale in December, 1943.[22]

The Little Saltee, meanwhile, had continued in the tenure of William White and still belonged to the residue of the Grogan-Morgan estate, being held in trust by, among others, Sir Henry Grattan Bellew, formerly of Mount Bellew,

Co. Galway, and later of Malahide, Co. Dublin, and Enniskerry, Co. Wicklow. William White apparently did not buy out the Little Saltee (the sale was, in fact, excluded by agreement with the Estate) and he is listed as tenant in various leases down to 1945, paying a rent of £35 a year, even though the holding had been declared "derelict" for many years. After William White's death his brothers and sisters, as his representatives, did not transact any business, and eventually the Little Saltee also was acquired by Michael Neale. Though the smaller island is not registered as having a legal owner in the Land Registry Office, Michael Neale is listed in Valuation Office records as the occupier. [23]

If possession is nine points of the law then he may now claim to be the owner of the Little Saltee too.

A page from the rent book of the Boxwell family showing rents paid by John Parle on the Great Saltee. Note the half-penny carried forward in the accounts!

1.   The Boxwells were the tenants for both islands, of Grogan of Johnstown Castle, to whose estate the Saltees belonged. "Martin Doyle" in his *Notes and Gleanings* records that a member of the Boxwell family obtained compensation from the Government about 1765 for cattle of which he had been plundered by American privateers who "frequently anchored there".

The Boxwells sub-let the islands first to the Furlongs, then to the Parles. I have already quoted from a return of the rental of lands forfeited by Cornelius Grogan after 1798. These lands included the Saltees; the tenant's name was S. Boxwell and the annual rent £34.2s.6d.

2.   Census of Ireland, 1659, National Library, Dublin. It has been suggested that the first Parle may have settled in Clongaddy and that the name of the place derived from his calling as a privateer: Clongaddy being an English form of "Gleann an Ghadai", the Glen of the Thief.

3.   1871 Census, Public Record Office, Dublin.

4.   *Topographical Dictionary of Ireland.*

5.   The inter-marriage of the Grogan and Knox families, resulting in the Knox-Grogan appellation, occurred early in the 18th century when Andrew Knox of Rathmachnee married Mary, fourth daughter of John Grogan, of Johnstown Castle. As well, in 1735, Katherine Knox, a daughter of this union married her cousin, John Grogan, M.P. of Johnstown Castle. Burke's *Irish Family Records* says the Grogan-Morgan family stemmed from these unions.

6.   *General Valuation of Ireland* by Richard Griffith.

7.   Records of the Valuation Office, Dublin.

8.   According to a marriage settlement in 1858, when the Earl of Granard married Jane Colclough Grogan-Morgan, the Saltee Islands, which had been left to her by her father, Hamilton Knox Grogan-Morgan, passed to the Earl. The settlement was not registered until August 4, 1890. (Book 37, p.164, no.1196, Registry of Deeds, Kings Inns).

9.   *Wexford County Guide and Directory,* by George Henry Bassett, Dublin, 1885.

10.   Yet it is related that one woman member of the Parle family never left the bigger island for 30 years.

11.   "Martin Doyle" in his *Notes and Gleanings* refers to the Parles' farming abilities: "There are now (1866) two small proprietors in this little townland of Clongaddy, the extent of which is but 93 acres. Mr. Francis Parle, who has the greater portion, is tenant to the Earl of Granard for the Little Saltee island, of which 50 acres are arable. Mr. Richard Parle, the larger proprietor, rents 12 acres at the distance of two miles from his residence. Since his proprietorship commenced he built a large and commodious house. All these men farm well and profitably..." Bassett added: "Little Saltee is held from year to year by Francis Parle of Clingarry (Clongaddy). There is a farmhouse on it, but it has not proved sufficiently attractive to induce Mr. Parle to make a home on the island." Thus the end of family habitation on the Little Saltee dates from before Francis Parle's tenancy, that is before 1855. Workers continued to live there until the beginning of the 20th century.

12.   Young Stephen Parle's death was not the only fatality on the islands. Another boy named Grant was killed while on a school outing from Wexford about 1917, and sixteen-year-old Dorothy Wallace, of Wexford, was killed in a fall from a cliff while visiting the Great Saltee with a bird-watching party in June, 1976.

13.   Bad weather and turbulent seas resulted in the death of a member of a rabbit-hunting party in 1907. Martin Pierce, then owner of Pierce's Foundry in Wexford, (and owner of the Great Saltee for a short time) and six others went out to the bigger island on June 5, 1907, planning to return about 5 p.m. But their boat was still high and dry at that time and they had to wait for another four hours before the incoming tide refloated the craft. In those few hours, however, the wind and the sea had risen. When shoving off in the boat, a wave struck it and drove it onto the rocks. All scrambled to safety, wading chest-deep through the water. The night was cold and the men shivered in their wet clothes. They had no food or drink. Fires which they managed to light went unseen on the mainland because of fog. They eventually found shelter in the old farmhouse, and made a fire out of the wooden staircase. In the morning they killed a heifer, which was among cattle grazing on the island and had a hot meal of soup and meat. By this time a search had been started for them and at 5 p.m. the party was taken off and brought to Kilmore. Martin Pierce, who had been unwell previously, had to be carried ashore and taken to Wexford that night (Thursday), suffering from the effects of exposure and exhaustion. He became seriously ill and died the following Saturday morning. He was forty-eight and had succeeded his brother Philip twelve years earlier as proprietor of the famous foundry that bore (and still bears) the family name. (See "Tragedy on the Saltee", *Kilmore Parish Journal,* 1976/77).

14.   Recollection of Mrs. Liz Jefferies, Ballask, Kilmore, whose father worked on the Little Saltee for the Whites.

15. "Gruts" were dehusked oat-grains used for human and animal consumption. Eggs were kept fresh by storing them in the "gruts".

16. The long winter nights on the exposed islands must have been difficult to endure. There were always indoor jobs to be done which helped to pass the time. Story-telling at the firesides, however, was the chief recreation. With the wind howling outside and the waves pounding on the cliffs and crags, it was inevitable that imaginations ran riot in those times. It is said that the noise of carts and farm machinery could often be heard on the Little Saltee when there were no carts or machinery to be seen. Will Culleton, the steward on the island, related that he often heard a mysterious knocking on the door of the farmhouse at the same time every night — but no one was ever seen there. Two other workmen, Dicky Barry of Neamestown, and Tommy Murphy of Kilturk, did discover the cause of the knocking at the door on another occasion. It turned out to be some of the farmyard ducks pecking at flies and woodlice on the warm woodwork!

17. Martin Pierce was the son of James Pierce of Kilmore, the man who established Pierce's Foundry in Wexford in 1839. On his death in 1868, his sons Philip and Martin assumed control of the firm which expanded and won acclaim all over the world for its farm machinery and implements. Philip died in 1895, and Martin was joined by another brother, John, in the management of the business.
   As we have seen (footnote three) Martin died in 1907, leaving John at the head of the concern. John died in 1926 and his son Philip B. took over the reins. The last of the Pierces to be associated with the Mill Road Works in Wexford. Philip B. is now retired, but is still active as Chairman of *The Irish Press Ltd.*, Dublin.

18. John Pierce registered as owner of Great Saltee, on November 30, 1922. Land Registry, cross ref. No. L.R.88/20612, Collection No. 138/224. The purchase agreement of 1910 was destroyed in the Four Courts fire of 1922. The Great Saltee was subject of an advance of £1,125 made by the Land Commission in February, 1922, under the Land Act of 1903. The original annuity was £39.7s.6d. while the annuity as revised under the Land Act 1933, was £25.16s.10d. The holding was put up for sale by public auction by the Land Commission, but the sale was abortive. It was after this that Martin Pierce came into possession.

19. Water must always have been a problem on the Saltees which, despite three wells on the bigger island and one on the smaller, were often "dry". John Weaving, naturalist and ornithologist, who spent many periods on the Great Saltee, discovered a pump here at the granite drinking trough and believes that the whole area under the road at this point is a natural storage reservoir, with the well situated on its overflow which then runs through the now silted-up duck-pond and down the steep little valley to the landing. A pond by the bungalow used to be fed by intermittent springs and another pond, near the throne, was fed by a better spring, but its overflow was led away from the house area to enter the deep field drains, possibly because this pond was continually fouled by washing gulls. John Weaving, who supplied this information, was founder of a bird observatory set up there in 1948. He first visited the islands in 1936. The observatory closed in 1963 because of lack of funds and support.

20. Instrument No.5030/30, registered in the Land Registry Office, Four Courts, Dublin, and dated January 18, 1930. The actual wording is: "Susan Pierce.... in consideration of £5 paid by Nicholas Brennan.... transferred the Great Saltee to him."

21. The tractor and threshing mill were ferried out to the Great Saltee, in sections, on a raft when the sea was calm.

22. From 1943, when Michael Neale, described as a chemical manufacturer, of 2, Green Park, Orwell Road, Rathgar, Dublin was first listed as registered owner of the Great Saltee, up to the present, the legal ownership of the island has changed several times, — but always remained in Neale's family. In 1944 the registered owner is given as John O'Neill, Ballinglee, Ballymitty, Co. Wexford, (farmer); in 1945 it is back in Michael Neale's hands again; and in 1948 both John O'Neill and Michael Neale are listed as registered owners. Michael Neale's name was originally O'Neill and he is John O'Neill's son.

23. Neale has underlined his claim to the Little Saltee in emphatic manner on at least one occasion — by shooting sheep which were put to graze there by a south Wexford farmer.

Chapter 10
´Prince` of the Saltees

The history of the Saltees in comparatively recent times is largely a sad story of dereliction, neglect, and litigation. When the Parle family finally withdrew from the Great Saltee in the first decade of the 20th century, no one took their place. The old farmhouse was boarded up, the fields became weed-grown, the stone walls and earthen boundaries began to crumble.

Cattle and sheep were still grazed on the two islands for some further years but this practice also ended. The rabbits and wild birds had the place to themselves once more and began to proliferate.[1] So did the bracken, the briars, and the wild flowers. Nature again had a free hand.

By 1907 Valuation Office records were already listing the house and the offices on the bigger island as "of no value" and "to be restored". The buildings on the Little Saltee had long since fallen into ruin. Yet the old farmhouse on the Great Saltee was not entirely useless. It still gave shelter to weather-bound visitors — to sportsmen hunting rabbits,[2] to ornithologists and botanists,[3] and occasionally to fishermen and divers.

While the Land Commission held the leasehold, attempts were made to dispose of the island, but there were no takers for some time — even though, as I have heard it stated, the Great Saltee could have been obtained at that time by merely taking over the Land Commission annuity. The island was offered to An Oige, but there were practical obstacles to the suggestion of setting up a hostel there.[4]

The new owner of the Great Saltee, Michael Neale, is a colourful character. The son of a farmer, John O'Neill, of Ballinglee, Ballymitty, Co. Wexford, his childhood and early manhood were spent on the family farm. He displayed unusual entrepreneurial abilities from an early age which apparently paid off when he went to England and accumulated some money there.

Returning to Ireland he set up a factory in Dublin which turned out, first, a cattle-feed substitute, and later a roof preservative. For almost four years after gaining possession of the Great Saltee in December, 1943, Michael Neale did not bother to visit his new domain. But one of his first acts after buying the island was to assume the title "Prince of the Saltees".[5] He afterwards

Below – The crest of "Michael, Prince of the Saltees".

Top right – The obelisk on the Great Saltee in honour of the "Prince" of the Saltees .

Left – The "throne" erected on the Great Saltee by "Prince" Michael.

91

disclosed that it had been his ambition, from the time he was ten years of age, to own the islands and to become "Prince of the Saltees". He said[6] he had got a registration for the title from the British Office of Heraldry;[7] that the Irish Government had refused to recognise the title on the registration of the birth of his son, and that consequently, when he threatened a High Court action, the Registrar-General acceded to his request and registered his son as a Prince.

Neale continues to use the title and won a small victory for its recognition when public bodies, notably Wexford County Council, started to address correspondence to "Prince Michael Neale". His actual "coronation" on the Great Saltee did not take place until July, 1956, by which time he had erected a stone throne, an obelisk and a flag-staff for the "royal" colours.

The obelisk[8] bears a plaque with Neale's likeness in profile and several inscriptions, while the chair carries a coat of arms showing a shield held by two mermaids, each of its quarters containing a different species of bird. Below the coat of arms is an inscription which runs: "This chair is erected in memory of my mother to whom I made a vow that one day I would own the Saltee Islands and become the first Prince of the Saltees. Henceforth my heirs and successors can only proclaim themselves Prince of these Islands by sitting in this chair fully garbed in the robes and crown of the Islands and take the Oath of Succession. Michael the First."

Beyond erecting these objects and attempting to plant trees, Neale has done little with the islands since he acquired them. In the 1940's, however, his legal battles with Wexford County Council over non-payment of rates on the islands focussed attention anew on the Saltees. These legal tussles began when the County Council sued Neale in May, 1945, for £41.8s.6d. for rates due up to March 31 of that year on the Great Saltee. The case was heard in the District Court and the D.J. gave a decree for £40.11s.11d. and costs, disallowing 16s.7d. rates due on buildings which were said to be "down". Neale appealed to the Circuit Court in June, 1945, and the Circuit Court Judge reversed the decision of the District Justice.

In March of the following year, the Wexford County Manager, Thomas D. Sinnott, instructed the County Council's solicitor to institute proceedings against "Mr. Prince Michael Neale" for the recovery of rates due on the Great Saltee. Neale, on receipt of this new demand for £139.7s.2d., replied through his secretary, saying he did not owe this money. The County Manager then issued a Civil Bill, which came before the Circuit Court in May, 1947, for £43.10s.3d. due for rates on the Great Saltee for the year ended March 31, 1946. This Civil Bill was dismissed, with costs awarded to Neale.

The County Manager did not give up, however. In the High Court on July 9, 1947, in an appeal, he was awarded a decree for £42.13s.0d. against Neale, the Judge holding that he (Neale) was in occupation of the Great Saltee, despite eloquent testimony by the defendant that he derived no benefit from ownership of the island. It was during the hearing of this appeal in Wexford that Neale disclosed some of his ambitions and plans for the Great Saltee. "I intend to develop the island something similar to Monte Carlo," he is reported as saying.[9]

"I was in Monte Carlo a short time ago and I am convinced I can develop the Saltee Island on similar lines. The only way I could develop it is by employing aeroplanes and it is my intention to use helicopters which I have seen used to a great extent in England during the war.... In the right sense of the word I bought the island when I was ten years of age although I could not pay for it then. It was an ambition of mine and I was determined to buy it. I was reared in very poor circumstances and it was my ambition to own these islands since I was ten and to become Prince of the Saltees.... I have always held that neither the Irish Government nor the British Government have any jurisdiction over the Saltee Islands except by force.... If the birds were never there, I would still have bought the island. I did not buy it for tillage because I did not think it could be tilled with profit. I heard Mr. Francis grew potatoes there for export and that people hostile to England burned the boats... I will develop the island when the coming war with Russia is over. I will spend a considerable amount on it then....."

By this time, according to Wexford County Council, Neale owed them £219.17s.10d., less £41.8s.6d. not recoverable and £42.13s.0d. on foot of a decree already obtained. But Neale still refused to pay a penny. In May, 1949, Wexford County Council lodged a decree with the Sheriff of Co. Dublin for levy but this was returned endorsed "No goods" by the Under-Sheriff who attempted service. Beyond some questions asked at a meeting of Wexford County Council in October, 1957, when it was agreed that Neale be written to and asked to pay the rates on the Saltees, the legal battle seems to have petered out. Has Michael Neale won?

Whatever about his long-term plans for the islands, Neale's more immediate moves to reduce the rabbit numbers led to considerable controversy. After an attempt in 1949 to grow thousands of conifers and shrubs on the Great Saltee failed — mainly because of the choking bracken but also as a result of the depradations of the rabbits — Neale declared war on the rodents. He first released two ferrets on the islands, but these concentrated on killing rats before succumbing to their first Saltee winter. Next, about a dozen foxes were transported to the island. These had been caged together for some time before being flown to the island and, as a result, all were infected with distemper and died soon after release.

Then came the cat air-lift. Neale obtained forty-six cats from an R.S.P.C.A. home. When flown to the Great Saltee and released from the plane — with a certain amount of publicity — both the R.S.P.C.A. and the Irish Society for the Protection of Birds joined in a widespread campaign of protest, the one condemning the cruelty to the cats, the other the threat to the birds posed by the cats.

Letters of protest from people in both camps poured in to the Irish newspapers. Questions were asked in the Dail. Eventually a task force of several Gardai, a veterinary surgeon, and a neutral observer went out to the island to see conditions for themselves. The vet was to report on the state of the cats, the Gardai were there to catch any that seemed to be suffering. Not a cat — least of all a suffering one — was seen, and the task force returned empty-handed. The case of the Saltee cat-lift soon faded from the news reports.

But the cats survived, for a time. Some of the more domesticated of them, which were unlikely to withstand the rigours of outdoor living, gathered round picnic-parties and found new homes ashore. The remainder flourished and a visitor to the island at the time reported that he had never seen cats in better condition. Sources of food were plentiful. They wiped out nearly all the remaining rats, then started killing puffins. Nature, however, has a way of redressing imbalances. When the cats had litters, few if any of the kittens survived their first winter, being too light to kill rabbits, the only food available at that season. Since the cats did not therefore multiply, they died out in approximately eight years. Once more the rabbits began to proliferate. [10]

In 1962 myxomatosis was introduced to the Great Saltee. This had drastic results, not only on the rabbits but also on the bird-life and on conditions generally. The rabbits normally kept the fields closely cropped. The absence of rabbits saw a return of weeds and rank growth. The ground-loving birds suffered – and so too did bird-watchers. Even walking across the fields became difficult. Yet the rabbits have survived. Every seven years or so there is a fresh outbreak of myxomatosis which kills thousands of the little animals. But some anti-disease strain conquers and they fight back, multiplying as only rabbits can, and become as numerous as ever.

As the rabbit was introduced to the Saltees in the Middle Ages, probably by the Tintern monks as a source of food and skins, and as the brown rat, which is again numerous on the bigger island, [11] arrived from a wrecked ship, the only indigenous land mammal on the Saltees is the pigmy shrew. Otters visit the islands occasionally and grey seals now breed there! [12]

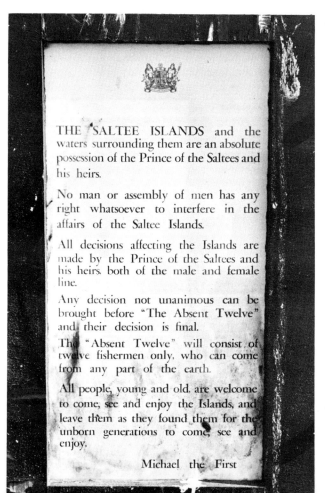

Left – The notice which confronts the visitor on landing on the Great Saltee.

FOOTNOTES – CHAPTER 10

1.   The rabbits became so plentiful that, on one's approach, whole fields seemed to be moving with them. They also became quite tame, scarcely bothering to scatter on man's approach. Inevitably the professional rabbit-catchers descended on the islands and thousands of rabbits were netted and snared. The war years of 1939-45 placed a premium on rabbit meat and they fecthed 1s.6d. a pair. Saltee rabbits were particularly tasty for some reason.

A lightshipman stationed for some years on the Coningbeg lightvessel said he frequently rowed the three miles to the Great Saltee to procure supplies of rabbits for cooking. "They were better than any chicken" he added.

2.   See footnote 3, previous chapter, on mishap to rabbit-hunting party in 1907.

3.   Robert Lloyd Praeger visited the islands in 1913, and described them in his book *The Way that I went.*

4.   John Weaving, a member of the Executive Committee of An Oige, was the only member acquainted with the island and to oppose setting up a hostel there even though, as he relates, all his inclinations were to get An Oige to take over the island and have himself appointed as warden.

5.   Neale was not the first to proclaim himself head of the Saltees. In 1919, in a facetious ceremony on the island, John Pierce was "crowned" King of the Saltees. Misfortune overtook the "royal" party when picnic baskets, champagne and silverware were lost overboard from their boat in landing.

6.   This was during a High Court Hearing in Wexford (in July 1947) of an appeal by the Wexford County Manager, Thomas D. Sinnott, against a Circuit Court decision by which a claim for rates on the Saltees made against Michael Neale was dismissed.

7.   Following publications of these remarks by Neale, the Garter King of Arms, Algar Howard, of the College of Arms, Queen Victoria St., London E.C.4, wrote a letter (*Evening Herald,* Dublin, July 16, 1947) stating that, as far as the College of Arms was concerned, Neale did not obtain any registration of a title there.

8.   After the erection of obelisk and throne on the Great Saltee, a grammatical error was discovered in one of the inscriptions. The sculptor was rushed from Dublin, taken out to the island, corrected the mistake, and returned home, all in the same day.

9.   *The Free Press* Wexford, July 12, 1947.

10.   The proliferating rabbits received some assistance during Claude Francis' tenure. A big buck rabbit became well known to the workmen on the Great Saltee and whenever he was caught in a snare they immediately freed him again. John Weaving recalls an occasion in May, 1943, when a rabbit's squeal cut short a conversation he was having with the farm-hands. "It's the big buck" cried one of them and they all raced to release him unharmed, lest the stock, and thereby their diet and income, disimprove!

11.   Thomas H. Mason (in his *Islands of Ireland,* 1936) described how two rabbit-trappers killed 157 rats in three days in the Great Saltee by the simple expedient of leaving scraps of food under a propped-up door taken off the hinges and jerking away the prop to crush the rats underneath.

12.   Douglas Deane, of Belfast Museum, in 1957 observed three young seal pups on the Great Saltee which he estimated to have been far too young to have swum across St. George's Channel from the Pembrokeshire coast where it was believed the seals bred.

Chapter 11
The Saltees in Verse and Song

"There is something about a small island" wrote R. M. Lockley, "that satisfies the heart of man". From such satisfaction springs the praise of many poets and song-writers who have extolled the mystic beauty of the Saltees down the years.

A long poem by R. D. Webb entitled, "The Mountain of Forth",[1] mentions, among numerous south Wexford landmarks and historic places, St. Patrick's Bridge and the Saltees:

"The causeway that St. Patrick built,

to march across the seas

The dashing of the wild waves

against the wild Saltees."

Webb was a nephew of Jacob Poole, of Growtown, best remembered for his collection of words and phrases in the Forth and Bargy dialect.

Patrick Joseph McCall, who could be called a Wexfordman by adoption, wrote several ballads and songs about south Wexford and refers to the Saltees in some of them. McCall penned much of his work amid the sandhills of Ballyteigue Burrow, and brings in numerous names of local places in his verses. Here is the first stanza of his "Wexford Fishing Song";[2]

The red sun rolls down over Ballyteig's waters,

And the Saltees grow misty and grey;

At home on the mainland our wives and our daughters

Are wishing good luck to the day!

With a west wind long blowing, our nets filled o'erflowing

From a shoal that broke under our lee;

Then raise high a chorus, the way lies before us

With a boat full of spoil from the sea!"

Even more popular is McCall's "Sailing in the Lowlands Low" which is sub-titled, "A smuggler's song"[3] and which has as its locale the waters round the Saltees. It mentions Bannow, Fethard, and the Hook, and in the last verse pictures the smuggler, after leaving his live cargo of twenty young "Wild Geese" in Flanders, returning with a cargo of contraband wines:

"Pray, holy Brendan,

Turk nor Algerine,

Dutchman nor Saxon may sink us!

We'll bring Geneva

Rack and Rhenish wine

Safely from the Lowlands Low!"

In "Songs of the Wexford Coast" a priceless collection made by the late Father Joseph Ranson, there are references to the Saltees and other coastal places; in "The Wreck of Kinsale" (which went down near Hook Head) and in "Paul Jones", (which tells the story of the running fight between "The Black Prince" commanded by Jones and a British man-o'-war).

Here is a verse from "Paul Jones":

The morning breaks o'er the Channel

wave as the stranger ship sails on,

With yards braced square before the

gale in the grey of early dawn.

The Channel breeze meets th' ebbing

tide that boils round Conneymore;

The mist lies heavy on the land

from Fethard to Carnsore."

Local poets, too, have written about the islands and their ballads help to chronicle local events and characters. Mike Flynn, of Kilmore, mentions the Saltees in his ballad about Ballyteigue[4] and describes the cries of the seagulls as they wing their way home.

"On the great Saltee Islands now dim in the twilight,

Like two fairy kingdoms afloat on the foam".

The magic of the islands inspired them all. For surely there is magic and mystery about the Saltees as they lie brooding on the horizon. They have withstood the onslaught of time, of wind and of wave. They have seen the brief efforts of man to conquer and subdue, and have watched him ultimately retreat to the mainland.

They hold their secrets of the past within themselves, as if reluctant to disclose them, and they remain, desolate, immutable and mysterious, as they have been from the beginning. Their overwhelming effect is one of peace — may they always retain this precious attribute in our increasingly unpeaceful world.

FOOTNOTES – CHAPTER 11

1. Webb's long poem is reproduced by Griffith in his *Directory of Co. Wexford.*

2. Air "Poll Cearnuit", No.1129, in *The Complete Petrie Collection.* Music has also been put to this McCall song by my aunt, Mrs. Richard Egan, Scar, and by my cousin, Tom Williams, Taghmon.

3. Air, No.182, in Dr. Joyce's *Old Irish Folk Music and Songs* and *Songs of the Gael,* Series 1, p.80.

4. From an article titled "A Parish Full of Poetry" by Kevin Whitty in the *Kilmore Parish Journal* 1976/77.

APPENDIX

THE KEERAGHS

There are two other tiny islands not far from the Saltees which are worthy of interest. These are the Keeragh Islands, situated half a mile or so off the coast at Cullenstown. In area they are little more than two acres and one acre, respectively, but for all their insignificant size they have been the scene of some awesome shipwrecks.

Owing to their smallness and bleakness the Keeraghs were probably never inhabited on a permanent basis though there may have been sheep herds there during grazing seasons. The ruins of a house on the bigger island may be those of the building referred to by Rev. William Hickey ("Martin Doyle") who wrote in 1868:

"The grandfather of the present proprietor (Captain Boyse) built a hut on the larger of these two diminutive islands, in which he placed stores of potatoes, whiskey, wood, candles and matches, in case of any shipwrecked people arriving there at night. To the credit of the extreme honesty of the peasantry of that time, it gives us pleasure to record that nothing of those provisions was even stolen, though it was notorious that they were there, in an open space, only half a mile from the shore."

The Keeraghs' only recorded owner was the Boyse family of Bannow House. Richard Griffith, in his "General Valuation of Ireland" (1853) said the bigger island (comprising 2 acres, 1 rood and 13 perches) was owned by Thomas Boyse and that the house on it was vacant. Thomas Boyse, who incidentally was a close friend of Tom Moore the poet, died on January 15, 1854. The smaller island is only 1 acre, 1 rood and 14 perches in extent.

John O'Donovan, in his Ordnance Survey name-book, suggested that the Irish name for the Keeraghs was "Oileain na gCaerach" (Islands of the Sheep) but this can only be regarded as a guess since this part of Wexford was in no way an Irish-speaking area in the 1830s when O'Donovan did his survey-work.

The name is more likely to be Norse in origin but there are several versions which add to the confusion. In inquisitions during the reigns of James I and Charles I in the 17th century, we find the islands called "The Keraghes". On a map with a statistical survey of Wexford in the 19th century they are called "The Keroe Islands" — the "oe" ending, meaning "island", suggesting a Norse or Danish origin.

Rev. William Hickey, describing the Boyse mansion at Bannow, said it commanded "a beautiful view of the sea, the Saltee and Keroe Islands".

The two barren, exposed islets are best remembered as the scene of several shipwrecks. Here, in 1819, the "Demarara", carrying gold bullion, was wrecked and sank. One passenger, a Scotsman named Hugh Monro Robertson, and sixteen members of the crew were drowned. Their bodies were washed ashore at Cullenstown and buried in the ancient graveyard in the Cill Park near Cullenstown Castle. Monro's is the only tombstone there now, as the pillared memorial over the sailors' mass grave was broken many years ago. Indeed, one of the small stone pillars from the tomb was used as a weight on a harrow by a local farmer!

To this day, it is said, traces of gold dust from the "Demarara's" strongroom are found in the sands on the Keeraghs.

In January, 1847, the "Niobe", laden with Indian corn and meal for famine-stricken Ireland, was lost on the Keeraghs. She had been bound from New York for Cork and apparently had been driven off course by bad weather. On January 19, 1874, in a fierce storm, the Italian brig "Vittorisso G." was driven in past the Keeraghs and wrecked in Bannow Bay. The crew were saved by Duncannon life-boat which was brought overland for five miles and launched from Fethard on that occasion. The Fethard life-boat station was not established until 1886.

About this time also, the "King Arthur" was wrecked at Ballymadder — the hull was visible at low tide up to twenty-five years ago. The mate of the "King Arthur" survived by swimming ashore with his clothes tied in a bundle on his head and on top of the bundle sat his black cat.

The worst local disaster of all to occur on The Keeraghs was the wreck of the Norwegian schooner "Mexico" on February 20, 1914, and the subsequent loss of the Fethard life-boat and nine of her crew. The "Mexico" was driven into Bannow Bay in a bad south-south-west gale and lost her bearings. In putting about she was carried towards the South Keeragh island. Her plight was seen by Fethard folk and the local life-boat set out to help. But the fierce seas swamped the life-boat and smashed her on the rocks of the island. Only five of her fourteen crew-members managed to scramble ashore. Despite their plight these five brave men set about rescuing the crew of the "Mexico" and soon had all nine safely off the schooner and on the island. Two other members of the "Mexico's" crew had landed in a small boat at Cullenstown. From late afternoon on Friday until Monday morning, the fourteen men huddled on the gale-swept islet, without water and with little food. Attempts by life-boats from Dunmore East, Kilmore and Rosslare to rescue them failed over the next two days. One of the "Mexico's" crew died from exposure on Sunday morning and his body was covered with canvas and sods. The other thirteen knew they faced certain death unless rescuers came soon. They had nothing to eat except two small tins of preserved meat, and raw limpets. Their only drink was a little brandy and half a pint of wine which the "Mexico's" captain had with him.

On Monday morning the Dunmore East life-boat made another attempt to reach the men on the Keeraghs. There was still a heavy ground-swell after the gale and the life-boat could only anchor one hundred yards from the shore and fire a line ashore on a stick rocket.

A skiff was eventually veered down by line towards the shore but it was smashed on the rocks. The men on the island were able to salvage a lifebuoy from the skiff and in this two of them were dragged through the water to the life-boat.

Meanwhile the Rosslare life-boat had been towed to the scene by a Wexford tug. In a strong punt two of the crew, James Wickham and William Duggan, were veered down by line from the life-boat and got close enough to the rocks to drag two of the shipwrecked men aboard. The punt was then hauled back to the life-boat. Again Wickham and Duggan veered the little boat towards the rocks. This time she was flung against them and holed. The gap was plugged hastily with a loaf of bread inside some packing and they went on with the work of rescue. Four times they made the perilous trip to and from the rocks until all twelve stranded men were safely aboard the life-boat. The tug then took the two life-boats in tow to port.

Ireland, Britain and Norway lauded the life-boatmen and rescuers of Fethard, Rosslare, Wexford, Kilmore and Dunmore East and the Life-Boat Institution bestowed medals and certificates on many of those involved in this stirring sea drama. A monument to the Fethard crew stands in the village street in Fethard — and in the old graveyard at Cill Park, Cullenstown, there is the grave of Antonio Levi, the Portuguese seaman who died and was temporarily buried on the South Keeragh and whose body was later re-interred in consecrated soil.

As recently as 1930 the Keeraghs were still taking their toll of shipping. In that year the "Mount Blarey", a 200-ton, three-masted schooner from Plymouth was wrecked on these deadly little islands.

FISHING GROUNDS

No study of the Saltees and their surrounding waters would be complete without even a brief reference to the rich fishing grounds in the area.

The biggest fishing bank is the Nymph Bank, which extends along the coasts of Wexford, Waterford and Cork at a distance of 20 to 35 miles. It was discovered in 1736 by a Mr. Doyle, hydrographer to the British Admiralty and named by him after the 12-gun brig in which he was sailing when he made his discovery. This bank is rich in flat fish — plaice, whiting, turbot, etc.

Another bank, the East Bank, stretches from Black Rock south-west for six miles and is about six miles wide. Another good ground lies east of the Coningbeg lightship.

Lobster-fishing gave good returns until recent years, when over-fishing reduced catches, but Kilmore lobsters are still prized in the best eating-places in several countries. Some of the places where pots are shot have unusual names — Scraff, Bokers, Dickeen and Madam Boyce.

PART TWO

The Birds of the Saltee Islands

Of the three hundred and ninety species of birds on the Irish List (that is, species which have been recorded at least once in Ireland in the last two hundred years) no less than two hundred and twenty three have been recorded on the Saltee Islands. This is remarkable in view of the small size of the islands and their isolation from the mainland, but more will be said on this later. In fact most of these species have been recorded on Great Saltee, but this is due mainly to lack of observations on Little Saltee and the broader range of habitats which are found on the larger island. Most of the breeding seabirds are common to both islands, as are many of the commoner breeding land birds, but intensive study of migration on Great Saltee during the 1950s and early 1960s (when there was a Bird Observatory) added a considerable number of species to the island's list. No comparable studies have been carried out on Little Saltee so its list is comparatively poor. All two hundred and twenty three species recorded on the islands are listed in the table on page 144 and an indication is given of each species' status, that is whether a species is rare or common in Ireland, a breeder or past breeder on the Saltee Islands, and whether it is vagrant, rare, scarce or common on the islands. It is hoped that this will enable visitors to the islands to determine whether their observations are of unusual or commonplace occurrences: if the former, the author of this part of the book would be very pleased to hear of such occurrences.

The birds of the Saltee Islands can be divided into three main groups, the breeding seabirds, the resident or breeding land birds, and the passage migrants and other visitors. These three groups are treated separately in the ensuing chapters.

Chapter 12
The Breeding Sea Birds

To the many hundreds of people who visit Great Saltee each summer the breeding seabirds are undoubtedly the great spectacle of the island. As one sets sail from Kilmore Quay there is little indication of what lies in store. A few gulls are always flying about in search of scraps and fish offal, and the large black Cormorants and Shags can be seen flying to and from the islands, singly or in small groups. Further out a few Razorbills, Guillemots and Puffins are encountered, flying across the bow or past the stern, or swimming quickly away as the boat approaches them on the water. Sometimes they are taken by surprise and hastily dive to escape the oncoming boat. As you sail past Little Saltee you can see the white dots scattered about the green of the island which are Herring Gulls (and also Great and Lesser Black-backs) sitting on their nests or standing guard close-by. The passing boat does not disturb these and the small numbers in the air are birds making routine flights between their nests and their feeding areas. At the south side of the small island you can also see the flattened white areas and guano-burnt vegetation of the Cormorant colonies peopled by dense bunches of large black birds standing erect and surveying the passing boat. Cormorants do not now breed on Great Saltee so this passing view is the best most people get. Little Saltee is in fact one of the most important sites in Ireland for breeding Cormorants, holding nearly three hundred pairs: besides breeding in dense colonies on the gentle slopes above the low cliffs of Little Saltee they can be found in neat rows nesting along the tops of the old stone walls which criss-cross the bracken covered island.

As the boat slows down and approaches the anchorage off the Great Saltee landing place there is still little sign of the tens of thousands of seabirds which breed there. A Grey Seal or two or three, and occasionally a Basking Shark, appear near the landing place and cause a bit of interest, and sometimes excitement, among the island visitors as they transfer from the fishing boat to the small punt for the short journey ashore. An anxious Oystercatcher and a few Herring Gulls, which have made their nests too close to the landing place for their own comfort, are the first birds to greet the landing party. If you are interested in seeing large numbers of Herring Gulls you need only make your way carefully (both to avoid standing on nests and twisting an ankle on the boulders) along the shore to the left or the right of the landing place and you will encounter hundreds of nests. The first half of June is usually the best time as most of the nests then contain eggs or newly-hatched young. The parent gulls will call and protest and swoop very close to your head as they attempt to drive you away from their nests, and they will sometimes actually hit you with their feet, a wing tip, or even a well-aimed spattering of guano! The birds quickly settle after the intruder has passed, but it is as well not to dally too long in the colony or some eggs or chicks will be chilled from lack of brooding, while a cannabalistic gull or two could swoop in and take eggs and young while the parents are distracted by the human intruder. One of the island's largest Herring Gull colonies is spread right along the boulder beach from Sebber to The Ring, and in places there is an overspill to the top of the low boulder-clay cliff. Other colonies are scattered around the steep sea-campion and lichen-covered rock slopes above the rocky cliffs on the seaward side of the island, and in a couple of areas which were once fields but which are now overgrown with bracken. It is mainly in this latter type of habitat that one finds the attractive yellow-legged, slate-grey-backed Lesser Black-backed Gull mixed in with the Herring Gulls.

If your visit to the island is just a day trip you will probably not have more than five or six hours to see the birds, and though the island is small it is very easy to run out of time and have to leave without visiting important areas. It is in fact possible to walk right round the island in a couple of hours — although the going is fairly difficult in places where the bracken and brambles have overgrown the pathways — but if you want to have a good look at the seabirds it is best not to attempt this, but rather to make your way to some of the best spots and there sit down at a good vantage point and observe the thousands of seabirds engaging in their various activities. Probably the best ploy for the day visitor with limited time is to climb the steps from the landing place, follow the path past the old farmhouse and garden, walk up the Cordeline-fringed "Royal Mile" to the Throne, and then follow the cliff-top south-westwards. The first half mile or so takes one past a series of small bays and headlands where the cliffs are relatively low — on average about seventy feet — and here can be seen quite nice colonies of Kittiwakes, Razorbills and Guillemots, together with small numbers of Shags, a scattering of Fulmars, and some cliff-nesting Herring Gulls. There are nearly always Puffins here too, especially close to the Throne, but they are unpredictable birds and often most of them are either away at sea fishing or hidden in their burrows deep in the earthen slopes above the cliffs. It is usually necessary to be on the island early in the morning or late in the evening (or in foggy conditions) to see the Puffins at their best, when they congregate in masses on the slopes above the cliffs. The ground from the Throne south-westwards is, in places, quite treacherous as it is riddled with burrows: many of these are Puffins', many too are rabbits' (which have recovered considerably from the outbreak of Myxomatosis in 1960 or 1961), but some are the burrows of the nocturnal Manx Shearwater. The day visitor is unlikely to see this strange species which comes ashore only on the darkest of nights. It is an experience never to be forgotten to spend a night on the island and at two or three o'clock in the morning to hear the

Right – A view of part of the Gannet colony from the sea. This picture was taken in early July when many of the young Gannets were almost as big as their parents, but covered with cotton-wool down.

Below – An unusual view of the Gannet colony – from the sea by the Seven heads. The very white area on the left of the colony is where non-breeders loaf about painting the rocks with their guano. In recent years the Gannet colony has extended downwards almost to wave level and upwards to the summit of the hundred foot cliff. There is now a tendency to move to the right as the colony slowly expands.

Top – a breeding adult returns to its nestling after a fishing trip of perhaps 100 miles away. On landing the adult will regurgitate a fish of up to 8 oz. and feed the nestling.

Left – This gannet is using all its 'equipment' to slow it down from 40–50 m.p.h. to allow for a gentle drop to its nest. Note the outspread feet, the fanned tail, the wings that are being used to back-pedal.
The gannet unlike most birds has binocular vision which enables it to see forward, and this is a great asset when hunting.

island come alive with the weird crowing calls of the shearwaters as they return from fishing trips to the Bay of Biscay and wing their way strongly through the darkness to their burrows and their waiting mates or offspring.

It is best not to delay too long on this part of the island, interesting though it is, as more spectacular colonies lie further on. A short steep climb up a bracken crowded path takes one to the plateau of the southern summit and once reaching the top it is an easy walk of just a few hundred yards to one of the high rocky outcrops overlooking the Gannet colony and the great arc of high cliffs which sweep east from there and which are covered with thousands of birds – mainly Guillemots, Razorbills and Kittiwakes. It is worth spending a while here and viewing the majestic Gannets as they fly to and from their colony on the highest and most southerly cliff on Great Saltee. Their guttural calls rise and fall as they engage in courtship displays or warn off too-close neighbours, and this sound is heard against a background of other bird noises – the anxious deep-throated call of the Great Black-backed Gulls overhead, the whirring of wings of Razorbills which have their nests under nearby boulders, the murring calls of the Guillemots (in North America they are called Common Murres) from the cliffs below, and the "kittiwake, kittiwake" cries of the Kittiwakes echoing about the rocks and chasms. And of course there is the constant sound of the sea – the gentle wash of the swell on a calm day, or the thundering roar of heavy Atlantic waves breaking against the cliff base. This is a good place to sit and watch awhile. The birds quickly accept your presence and carry on with their chores of incubating their eggs, brooding their young, guarding their territories against their neighbours, warning off predatory gulls, keeping themselves as immaculate as possible by preening their feathers from time to time, courting their mates, flying out to sea and returning with food for their young, and so on. All these activities can be watched at close quarters from a good vantage point. But a word of warning: the cliffs are dangerous in places and it is best to confine yourself to areas of good solid rock when close to the edge.

After a while you could, if you wished, continue past the Gannet cliff. The coast swings north-west and after about three hundred yards the cliffs begin to give way to less beetling precipices and eventually, about half way back to The Ring, they become no more than boulder clay banks protected from the sea by storm beaches. It is possible to return to the landing place by following the coast around this way, but few birds, other than Herring Gulls, will be seen on this part of the island. It is better to climb the slopes of sea campion to the plateau again and return by the outward path. Great Black-backed Gulls will escort you all the way across the plateau for it is here that their main colony lies. Though much bigger than the Herring Gulls they seem more shy of humans and do not put on a brave show of trying to drive you away from their nests. When you get to the north end of the southern plateau there is, on a clear day, a breathtaking view of the northern two-thirds of the island, with Little Saltee beyond, and in the distance the mainland coast stretching from Kilmore Quay eastwards to Carnsore Point and the Tuskar light-house, and westwards to the long low peninsula of Hook Head with its ancient squat black and white light-house. By now time is probably running out and you need to allow at least twenty minutes to walk briskly from the plateau back to the landing place. However, if there is still time in hand you can have another look at the little bays on the way back to The Throne. Many of the birds will be in exactly the same position as earlier, but if the evening is advancing there is a good chance there will be more Puffins about. If you still have time it is worth sticking to the cliff top and proceeding past The Throne to a point opposite The Megstone, a high cone of rock separated from the island by a narrow channel. The top of this rock islet is so densely packed with Gannets and Guillemots it is a wonder the birds have space to raise their chicks let alone just stand there practically rubbing shoulders.

The itinerary outlined in the previous paragraphs will give the visitor with limited time a good view of the more impressive cliffscapes and bird colonies, and it is virtually certain that ten of the eleven species of breeding seabirds found on Great Saltee (the one unlikely to be seen being the Manx Shearwater) will have been seen well. As mentioned earlier the Cormorant is nowadays confined to the Little Saltee. Visitors who have little or no experience of seabirds may have a little difficulty identifying the various species: it is hoped that the bird photographs illustrating this book will be a help with this, and the following sections, treating in some detail each of the twelve seabird species of the islands, contain verbal descriptions of the birds in various stages of growth and plumage, as well as giving other information on their breeding biology and life cycle.

The table on page 147 gives an indication of the numbers of breeding pairs of seabirds on each island and the totals for the two islands. All species combined add up to about 30,000 pairs, that is about 60,000 breeding adults. Add to this the young birds produced each year — let us say an average of one young bird per pair (Fulmars, Manx Shearwaters, Gannets, Razorbills, Guillemots and Puffins lay only one egg while the others usually lay two to four eggs: allowing for loss of eggs and young through predation, infertility, disease and so on it is probably reasonable to assume that the less than one young per pair produced by the former group is compensated for by the more than one young per pair produced by the latter group).

The total number of seabirds on the island towards the end of the breeding season probably reaches 90,000. Many of the seabirds do not breed until they are three, four, five or even more years of age, so there is also a large contingent of immature birds floating about (both literally and figuratively) which will eventually return to their natal colonies to breed. Mortality among immature birds is high but even so a fair proportion of each year's batch of successfully reared young will survive and return to breed. If these are added to the late breeding season total of about 90,000 birds we end up with a population figure for the Saltee Islands of probably well over 150,000 birds. This figure is very large but nothing compared with T. H. Mason's estimate (given in *The Islands of Ireland*) of a staggering 2,500,000 to 3,000,000 birds. It is presumed that he was referring mainly to the auks, especially the Razorbills and Guillemots. A census carried out in 1969 and 1970 of virtually all the colonies of these two species on the coasts and islands of Ireland and Britain produced a grand total of only 721,000 breeding pairs. In light of this it is difficult to believe that up to three million birds could have been on the Saltees a mere forty years ago. Furthermore, if one takes all the habitat on the islands which is suitable, or potentially suitable for nesting auks and calculates its area (by taking a linear measurement of the shore-line and multiplying this figure by the average height of the cliffs/slopes, minus the height to which heavy spray usually reaches) there simply is not room for so many birds. The actual density works out at about 40 square inches per bird!

Nevertheless, though we must treat early estimates with some scepticism, there have undoubtedly been very significant changes in numbers of most species in this century. Little is known about the Manx Shearwater colony, though it is believed to have increased significantly in very recent years. The Gannet and the Fulmar are completely new colonisers (the latter not only of the Saltees but of Ireland since 1911), and the Cormorant has deserted Great Saltee and is now confined to the smaller island. The Great and Lesser Black-backed Gulls have probably increased somewhat, but the Herring Gull has done so enormously,* and it is probably safe to assume that the Kittiwake has also increased this century, in step with well-documented increases in many colonies around the coasts of Britain and Ireland — but its population appears to have levelled off somewhat in the last twenty-five years. The auks, the Razorbill, Guillemot and Puffin, are the birds which give most cause for concern. These are the seabirds which are most vulnerable to pollution of the sea, especially by oil spillages, and in recent years it has come to light that many thousands are drowned each year when they become entangled in drift nets deployed around the Irish coasts in summer, and in non-breeding areas around the Bay of Biscay and on the coasts of Spain and Portugal they also fall victim to drowning in fishing nets. On the Saltees a very serious decrease in Guillemot numbers occurred when large numbers died in the Irish Sea in autumn 1969. The deaths were probably caused by a combination of chemical pollution, stormy weather, stress during the moulting period, and a shortage of food. However, the numbers quickly returned to normal as immature birds which had been elsewhere that autumn came back to the colonies the following summer. In the longer term Puffins have probably decreased greatly this century. Photographs taken in 1912 show large numbers by their burrows in extensive colonies near The Throne, areas which are now largely deserted. This may be a case where a combination of predation by gulls (increasing as gull numbers have increased) and human disturbance (this very area is the one subject to greatest disturbance) has caused the decline in this attractive little seabird.

In the context of Ireland as a whole the seabird colonies on the Saltee Islands are placed well up in the "Top Ten", both in terms of absolute numbers of birds and diversity of species. Only four other cliff-type seabird colonies have over 10,000 breeding pairs of seabirds — Rathlin Island (Co. Antrim), Horn Head (Co. Donegal), and the Blasket Islands and Skelligs (both groups in Co. Kerry) — and only two of these (Rathlin and the Blaskets) have more breeding species: each has thirteen as opposed to the twelve found on the Saltees. There are a number of reasons why the Saltees hold such a major place among the seabird colonies of Ireland. The nature of the islands themselves, especially the larger one, with long stretches of cliffs of various kinds, boulder-strewn slopes, earthen slopes for burrowing seabirds, plateaux, boulder beaches, rocky outcrops for gulls, and so on — these various habitat types provide ideal

*These three gulls have declined recently, due to botulism.

nesting sites for the seabirds which have their own particular preferences. The islands are far removed from other suitable nesting islands and headlands: as one goes northwards along the Irish coast there are no suitable rocky headlands before Wicklow Head and Bray Head, sixty and more miles away, and these hold only small colonies. Lambay Island and to a lesser extent Ireland's Eye and Howth Head are the only seabird colonies of any size on the east coast. Westwards from the Saltees there is a good Kittiwake colony at Dunmore East and a scattering of breeding seabirds along the mainland cliffs of Co. Waterford, but it is not until one gets to The Old Head of Kinsale in Co. Cork, about one hundred miles south-west of the Saltees, that large numbers are again encountered. So the presence of very suitable habitats on the Saltees, which are in addition geographically isolated from other major areas of suitable habitats, cause seabirds to concentrate there in great numbers. Their own geographical position too, placed as they are near the southern entrance to the Irish Sea in St. George's Channel, makes the Saltees a very suitable place from which to exploit the large shoals of small fry, sand-eels, and the larger fish which prey on them. The strong tidal movements of oxygen- and plankton-rich waters in this south-east corner of Ireland bring an abundance of food within easy reach of the thousands of seabirds which launch forth from their nesting places in search of the fish so vital for their growing young and their own survival.

1. The Fulmar — *Fulmarus glacialis*

At first glance the Fulmar looks like the common Herring Gull, but on closer examination one sees the peculiar bill, apparently made up of several separate pieces and with tube nostrils extending along the top edge. The bird also has a dark eye with a sooty smudge of feathers around it, and has a heavy-looking head and thick neck. The upper-parts are a darker grey than those of the Herring Gull, and the protruding wing tips are darker still and lack the alternating black and white marks of the gull's. In flight the Fulmar is immediately recognised by its long stiff wings which it hardly flaps at all as it glides effortlessly about the cliff-face. The grey upper surface of the tail can also be clearly seen in flight: in the gulls the tail is completely white. In flight, also, one can see that the Fulmar's wing-tips lack the black and white of the Herring Gull's, and there is a fairly distinct whitish area at the base of the primary flight feathers. The colour of the bill is variable but yellow usually predominates, and tinges of blue and green are often present.

Young Fulmars, on hatching, are coated with an incredible amount of very soft fluffy pale grey down. They retain this down for much of the seven weeks it takes them to fledge, but as the adult-type feathers grow through towards the end of this period the down is quickly shed.

When fledged the young Fulmars go to sea and spend their first three or four years of life away from land. Then they start to take an interest in nesting activities and come ashore to "prospect" for suitable nesting sites. However, it seems to take them several more years to make up their minds where to nest as they don't usually lay until they are seven years old. On the Saltee Islands most of the Fulmars nest on bare earthen ledges on the boulder-clay cliffs and on the steeper slopes: often the nest site is sheltered by an overhanging

Left top – A Fulmar incubating its egg in a typical Saltee nest-site, an earthen ledge overhung by boulders.

Left below – A Manx Shear-water, just back from several days at sea, photographed by flash at night before it disappeared down its nesting burrow.

Right – A pair of Gannets by their seaweed nest in the colony at the south end of Great Saltee. The well-grown but still downy young bird behind and to the left belongs to another pair and is sitting just out of bill range. The bird in the background (top right) is a Razorbill.

boulder. Only one egg, completely white in colour, is laid and this is incubated for nearly eight weeks, by both parents taking turns of about five days each. The young are fed only once or twice a day, with fish offal and zooplankton regurgitated by the parents. Birds arriving at the nest site are greeted by the "on-duty" parent by much bill waving and loud gutteral cackling calls. Non-breeding Fulmars and "off-duty" birds often spend their time gliding about the cliffs. They are inquisitive birds and will glide to within a few feet of the observer to get a closer look. If the nest is approached both the adults and the young birds will defend themselves, with considerable force and accuracy, by firing a vile-smelling oily substance at the intruder.

On the Saltee Islands Fulmars are often present on the nest sites in November and December, and attendance at the colonies increases as the spring progresses. Laying usually begins in early May and continues into June. Accordingly, it is mid-August before the first young fledge, and many are still to be found on the ledges in early September. Away from the colonies the Fulmar ranges widely over the Atlantic, sometimes as far west as Labrador, and often far into the Arctic regions. The species does not usually wander south of the temperate regions.

Until about one hundred years ago Fulmars were confined, in Britain and Ireland, to the St. Kilda Islands in the Outer Hebrides. Then they began to expand their range and in 1911 nesting was first proved in Ireland, in Co. Mayo. One pair nested on the Saltee Islands, in 1929, and by 1950 there were twenty to twenty-five pairs. Ten years later there were at least fifty-five pairs, while now they are very firmly established with over 465 breeding pairs, the majority of these on Great Saltee.

Elsewhere in Ireland Fulmars are now nesting on most of the suitable islands and mainland cliffs of our coasts, and they are particularly numerous in Cork, Kerry, Clare, Mayo, Donegal and Antrim. Abroad, the Fulmar, separated into three sub-species, is found in both the Pacific and Atlantic Oceans — in the Kurils, Alaska and the Bering Sea; in the Atlantic, birds breed in Norway, Novaya Zemlya, Britain, Ireland, north-west France, the Faeroes, Iceland, Spitzbergen, Jan Mayen, Greenland, and islands in north-east Arctic Canada.

2. The Manx Shearwater — *Puffinus puffinus*

This species is the least numerous breeding seabird on the Saltee Islands, and even apart from this fact it is seldom seen, for it is found in the open only in the dark of the night. Day visitors to the islands could be forgiven for thinking that all the burrows were occupied by rabbits and Puffins, but some contain nesting Shearwaters. The change-over of the incubation and the feeding of the young takes place on moonless or cloudy nights between 23.00 and 02.00 hrs. and it is possible to locate incoming birds by their weird crowing calls and the thump of their bodies as they land. One can then pick out the birds with a strong lamp, before they scuttle down into their burrows. Manx Shearwaters are about fourteen inches long, completely black on the upper-parts and pure white underneath. The bill is black, has small tube nostrils, and there is a wicked hook at the tip. The legs are set far back (making it difficult for the bird to get about on land) and are a mixture of black and pink. The bird is at its best on the wing: it is a superb glider and uses every little updraught of air from the wave-crests to give it buoyancy as it shears and twists its way at high speed over the sea, showing alternately its flashing white underparts and black upperparts. It usually stays well away from land in day-time but parties (indeed sometimes continuous streams of several thousand) can be seen rounding some of the more prominent headlands, and a few are sometimes seen from boats going to and from the Saltees.

The young Manx Shearwaters are covered with grey down from the time of hatching, but they look like their parents when they are ready to leave their burrows at about ten weeks of age. During their first weeks of life they are brooded by one of the parents and they are fed on regurgitated small fish — pilchards, sprats, etc. By the time they are seven or eight weeks old they are enormously fat and weigh about twice as much as their parents. They are then deserted and they live off their fat for two or three weeks before taking to the sea at night.

Adult shearwaters return to the colony quite early in the spring, but egg-laying does not start until the end of April or early May. A single large white egg is laid in a chamber at the bottom of the nesting burrow. As with the Fulmar the incubation and fledging period is very long — as much as seventeen weeks — and many young are still at the colony at the end of August. In September the birds migrate rapidly south-westwards to their wintering grounds off the east coast of South America: ringed birds have been known to complete this 5,000 miles journey in as little as eighteen days. Sometimes birds are driven far off course by storms and there is an instance of a Welsh Manx Shearwater ending up in south Australia. Young birds begin to return to their natal areas in the summer of their second year, but they usually do not start to breed until they are five years old.

It is not known when the Saltees were first colonised by Manx Shearwaters, but they were certainly breeding there at the end of the last century. They were found nesting on Little Saltee early this century, but, so far as is known, none now nest there. Because of the birds' nocturnal habits and their choice of nesting site it is very difficult to estimate their numbers. Various authors have suggested there are not more than fifty pairs nesting on Great Saltee, but the present writer believes there may now be up to 150 pairs.

The main strongholds of the Manx Shearwater in Ireland are the islands off the Kerry coast — the Skelligs, Puffin Island and the outer Blaskets. On Puffin Island there are believed to be over 10,000 pairs. Other sizeable colonies are found on the Copeland Islands (Co. Down), Rathlin Island (Co. Antrim) and islands off the coasts of south Mayo and north Galway. In Wales there are huge colonies on two of the Pembrokeshire islands and on Bardsey Island, while in Scotland the Isle of Rhum and adjacent islands have very large numbers. The species is also found in south Iceland, the Faeroes, Brittany, and on the Azores and Madeiras.

3. The Gannet — *Sula bassana*

The Gannet is our largest seabird, being three feet long and with a wing-span often over seven feet. The adult bird is snowy white all over, with the exception of black wing-tips and a suffused yellow colouring about the head. The bird has binocular vision and the pale blue-grey eyes have a strange staring quality. The bill is long and dagger-shaped and is a pale bluish-grey in colour with thin black horizontal lines extending back to the gape and below the eyes. The feet are dark grey and have rather intriguing little greenish lines running along the toes. The wings are long, narrow and pointed, and the tail is also long and pointed. Out at sea and at a distance the Gannet looks about twice the size of a Herring Gull, and the gleaming white plumage and black wing-tips are the most notable features. The birds are often seen off the coast in summer, plunging from heights of up to one hundred feet and diving into the water like spears, wings closed, in pursuit of shoals of mackerel or herring.

On hatching, young Gannets are tiny and helpless and are covered with leathery-looking blackish skin. They soon grow a coat of white cotton-wool-like down and this they retain until they are almost as big as their parents. Then the feathers grow through and the down is gradually lost. The Gannet's first feathers are dark brown with small white speckles: the rump is the only pale area. It takes the immature birds four years to attain their adult-like plumage, and both at sea and at the colonies birds in intermediate stages of plumage may be seen. The upper surfaces of the wings are last to become white.

Gannets nest in dense colonies, generally on steep rocky cliffs. The nests, made of rotting seaweed, and often incorporating all kinds of flotsam and jetsam (including pieces of bright nylon fishing nets), are placed on ledges within striking distance of neighbouring nests. The solitary, rather small egg is laid in April: when fresh-laid it is pale blue but rapidly becomes chalky white and progressively dirtier. Both parents incubate the egg for over six weeks, and it takes a further thirteen weeks for the young to fledge. While growing, the young are fed several times a day on regurgitated fish, often up to half a pound in weight. At the end of August and in early September the fat youngsters jump off the cliffs and glide down to the sea and swim away from the colony. It takes several days for them to lose enough weight to be able to take off and fly properly. Young Gannets from Ireland and Britain move south to the coast of west Africa, and some also move into the Mediterranean. Adults usually move no further south than the Bay of Biscay and Iberia, presumably so that they can return quickly to the colonies in January and February. A great amount of impressive courtship display is seen leading up to egg-laying, and indeed right through the breeding season, and while at the colony Gannets are extremely vocal, uttering a long series of gutteral croaks.

Of the three Irish Gannet colonies the one on Great Saltee is the smallest and most recently established. Birds were first seen "prospecting" in the late 1920s and in 1929 two pairs nested. However, the colony was slow to establish itself and it was not until 1954 that it began to increase significantly. By 1960 thirty to forty pairs were nesting and ten years later there were 165 breeding pairs. Since 1970 the population has continued to increase, reaching over 600 pairs by 1986, and establishing a new colony on The Megstone.

The other Irish colonies are situated on Little Skellig, Kerry, and Bull Rock, Cork. The former has about 22,000 breeding pairs and is probably the second largest in the world: the Bull Rock has over 1,500 pairs and the colony is increasing. Our Gannet is confined to the North Atlantic and colonies totalling nearly thirty in number are situated in Newfoundland, the Gulf of

St. Lawrence, Iceland, the Faeroes, Norway, north-west France, Britain and Ireland. The total population approaches 265,000 pairs.

4. The Cormorant — *Phalacrocorax carbo*

This species is one of the more familiar seabirds and is found not only around our coasts and estuaries but often far inland on lakes and rivers. Indeed, there are several places in Ireland where Cormorants actually nest in trees on lake islands, and this is a common practice in south-east Europe. The adult bird is large (about three feet long) and black, but seen close-to and in sunlight one notices a bronze sheen on the wings and a blue sheen on the body plumage. The bill is long and hooked and yellowish in colour, while the legs are black. A distinctive white face and chin patch, as well as its larger size, separates the Cormorant from its close relative, the Shag. During the breeding season the adults also have a white patch on each flank, and this is particularly noticeable in flight. The chicks are blind and naked when they hatch, and are not unlike those of the Gannet, but they quickly grow sooty black down. As they near fledging this down is replaced by dull brown feathers on the upper-parts and off-white on the under-parts.

When flying over the sea Cormorants usually fly low and straight, with strong regular wing-beats: when several are travelling together they usually fly in single file. However, when flying over land birds often reach considerable heights and groups often form echelons, like geese. On the water they are expert swimmers and divers and can remain under the surface for ninety seconds or more, pursuing the fish on which they feed. They have voracious appetites and gorged birds can frequently be seen perched on rocks, break-waters and so on, with wings stretched to dry. Cormorants are generally very silent, but at the nesting colonies utter deep gutteral calls.

Although common and widespread in Ireland Cormorants nest in only about forty colonies, and of these only four or five hold over a hundred breeding pairs. One of the largest colonies is situated on the Little Saltee where nowadays nearly 300 pairs nest. On Little Saltee the birds build their substantial nests of seaweed and bits of vegetation on rocky outcrops, and even along the tops of old dry-stone walls. Elsewhere nesting sites vary considerably: in some places the birds build on sheer cliffs, in others on storm beaches just out of reach of the waves and, as mentioned already, some even nest high up in trees. The female lays three or four chalky white eggs and these are incubated by both parents for just over four weeks. The young then take about seven weeks to fledge, but they usually stay near the colony for several more weeks before moving away to sea. In the autumn there is a general dispersal away from the colonies, but few birds move more than one hundred miles from their native area.

While the Cormorant is restricted to Little Saltee nowadays it was a common nester on Great Saltee in the last century and the early part of the present one. By 1943 the Great Saltee population had declined to about twelve pairs and by the end of that decade none was left. It is believed that disturbance caused by farming activities may have been the main cause of the decline. For some unknown reason one pair of Cormorants did nest on Great Saltee in 1973.

Top — A flight of Cormorants leaving their loafing place on the low cliffs at the seaward side of Little Saltee. The cliffs on this island, as typified in this photograph, are too low for Guillemots, Kittiwakes and other cliff-nesters which abound on Great Saltee.

Below — Shags are early nesters and by mid-summer most have reared their young. Here a large gathering of adults and recently fledged young rest on one of their favourite rocks just off the south side of the Great Saltee. They are accompanied by a small group of Puffins on the bottom left slope, and a solitary Great Black-backed Gull on the right.

The Cormorant is one of the most widespread of all birds, being found on all continents except South America. It breeds in north-eastern North America and western Greenland, Iceland, the Faeroes, north-west Russia, Scandinavia, the south Baltic and North Sea coasts of Europe, Britain, Ireland and Brittany. Then it occurs again in south-east Europe and in the Black Sea, and eastwards across Asia to Japan, and southwards to southern India and China. Cormorants also breed in the Ethiopian and Australasian regions. The total population of Britain and Ireland is over 10,000 pairs, of which nearly 4,000 pairs are found in Ireland.

5. The Shag – *Phalacrocorax aristotelis*

The Shag is a close relative of the Cormorant and is very like it in general appearance. It can be distinguished from the Cormorant by its smaller size and more slender shape, and its lack of white on the face and chin. The Shag does not have the white flank patch found in breeding adult Cormorants, and the black plumage has a bottle-green sheen all over instead of the blue and bronze sheens of the Cormorant. In early spring the Shag develops a prominent crest which curls upwards from the crown, but this adornment disappears by mid-summer. Immature Shags look just like small immature Cormorants and can usually be distinguished only by the experienced ornithologist. In flight the Shag proceeds with more rapid wing-beats than the Cormorant, and its neck is usually held more out-stretched. Unless forced by storms to seek the shelter of enclosed bays and estuaries the Shag much prefers the open rocky coasts: it is virtually never seen on inland lakes and rivers. Sitting on their nests Shags have a reptillian look as they stare with pale green eyes at the intruder. When opening their bills in a threat gesture they display a bright yellow gape. The newly-hatched and growing young Shags are very similar to young Cormorants.

This species is a more secretive nester than the Cormorant, and usually builds under cover of boulders, in rock crevices, and on ledges of caves. The nest is constructed of rotting seaweed and its presence can often be detected by the deposits of white excreta outside the entrance. The presence of a bird on the nest is often indicated by a hissing sound from within the nesting cavity. Shags often lay very early in the spring – as early as the end of February – but the laying period is extended so that one can find newly-fledged young at a colony at the same time as partially incubated eggs. However, by mid-July most of the young have taken to the sea or are sitting on rocks in groups at the base of the cliffs. The eggs, like the Cormorant's, are chalky white and usually number three. These are incubated by both parents who keep them warm by placing them on top of their feet, and they hatch after four or five weeks. It takes the chicks a further eight weeks to fledge and leave the nest, and for another three weeks or so they are still fed by their parents.

Shags breed on both the Saltee Islands, but numbers fluctuate considerably. Nowadays about 100 pairs nest on Little Saltee, while 450 pairs usually nest on Great Saltee. It is said that 500 pairs nested on the big island in 1942, and about that time none was nesting on Little Saltee. When the birds leave the colonies in late summer they disperse around the coasts of Ireland – from the Saltees not usually further west than Cork or further north than Down or

Antrim; some cross to the other side of the Irish Sea. The adults tend to be more sedentary than the young birds.

Elsewhere in Ireland there are only three or four Shag colonies as large as the Saltee ones, but there are over 100 small colonies scattered all round the coast, wherever the habitat is suitable, and single pairs are often encountered nesting away from these colonies. The total Irish population is probably close to 3,000 pairs. Outside Ireland the Shag is confined to the western Palaearctic region, being found in Iceland, the Faeroes, the coast from north-west Russia to southern Norway, north-west France, west Iberia, Morocco, and in the Mediterranean and Black Sea.

6. The Great Black-backed Gull — *Larus marinus*

The Great Black-back is the largest gull found in western Europe. The adults are unmistakable because of their large size and jet black wings and mantle. The birds measure two and a half feet from bill tip to tail tip and have a wing-span of five feet. Apart from the black on the wings (there are white spots on the tips) and mantle the plumage of the adult is all white. The massive bill is yellow with a red spot at the tip of the lower mandible, the iris of the eye is pale yellow, and the legs and feet are fleshy pink. Immature birds also have pinkish legs but otherwise are totally unlike their parents in colouring and can best be identified by their large size. In general appearance they are very like immature Lesser Black-backed and Herring Gulls — that is, a rather non-descript speckled brown — but they tend to have paler heads and darker tail tips than the two smaller species. As they get older they progressively become whiter on the body and blacker on the wings and mantle, and they acquire their full adult plumage when four years old. The bill and eyes are dark until about the third year after hatching. The call of the Great Black-back, uttered frequently both at the breeding colonies and at feeding sites, is much deeper than that of other gulls, and is a good identification guide.

Great Black-backed Gulls are the lords of the seabird colonies. They choose the highest vantage points on rocky stacks and outcrops on which to make their nests of dried grasses and other plants. Often the nest is close to a rock which the off-duty parent uses as a vantage point. The clutch of three eggs, coloured pale greenish-grey and dotted with large brown and black spots, is laid mainly during the latter half of April, and the chicks hatch about four weeks later. They are covered in soft fluffy down of pale speckled grey-brown and after a couple of days they leave the nest and seek the greater security of the surrounding bracken or other long vegetation. If an intruder approaches the parents call anxiously and the young birds "freeze" in the dense cover and are very hard to locate. The parents also attempt, sometimes successfully, to drive the intruder away by making low swoops at the head. However, they seldom strike human intruders. The chicks take seven or eight weeks to fledge and they can be identified as Great Black-backs by their large size by the time they are five or six weeks old. Their heads have white down with large blackish spots and this also helps to distinguish them from the young Lesser Black-backs and Herring Gulls.

During the breeding season the Great Black-backs get most of their food from the immediate vicinity of the colony, preying on the eggs and young of other seabirds, and they will kill adult Puffins and Manx Shearwaters, skinning their victims with one or two sharp head-shakes. They will also take rabbits, shellfish, carrion and almost any kind of meaty food they can find. In winter and away from the colonies they frequently inhabit rubbish dumps, sewage outfalls and abattoirs, and at sea will follow fishing boats for the gutted offal thrown overboard.

This large gull nests on both of the Saltee Islands and nowadays has a total population of over 500 pairs, divided equally between Great and Little Saltee.* Thirty years ago there were less than a hundred pairs on the two islands, but it is probable the increase will slow down now due to lack of space. The southern summit plateau of Great Saltee holds the greatest concentration. Elsewhere in Ireland only a few islands in Kerry, Galway and Mayo hold comparable numbers, but the species is widely distributed around the rocky coasts of Ireland, and there are also a few small colonies on lake islands in the west of Ireland. Irish nesting Great Black-backs are fairly sedentary and seldom move more than 100 miles south of their breeding areas, but in winter birds from northern Scandinavia, Russia and Iceland move south to British and Irish waters. The species also breeds in Greenland, the Faeroes, Bear Island, Spitzbergen, in the Baltic, in north-west France, and on the east coast of North America from Labrador to New York State. During the present century the Great Black-back has increased greatly in numbers and has extended its breeding range accordingly.

7. The Lesser Black-backed Gull — *Larus fuscus*

This species is a small, gentler-looking version of the Great Black-back, with slate-grey wings and mantle and very distinctive bright yellow-ochre legs and feet. The black tips of the wings, with white spots, contrast quite clearly with the slate-grey of the rest of the upper surface, while in the Great Black-back there is no difference in shading. The yellow eye of the Lesser Black-back can be seen to have a bright orange ring around it. Immature birds are very difficult to separate from immature Herring Gulls, but in the hand the experienced ornithologist can identify the two species by markings on the secondary flight feathers of the wing. However, as the Lesser Black-back matures it becomes more readily identifiable as it develops its dark grey back and yellow legs. The calls are not as deep as those of the Great Black-back but cannot easily be distinguished from those of the Herring Gull.

Unlike the Great Black-backed and Herring Gulls, the Lesser Black-back is almost exclusively a summer visitor to Ireland, arriving in mid-February and departing at the end of September or early October for wintering grounds in Spain, Portugal and north-west Africa. Sometimes large gatherings can be seen on the south coast prior to departure, and in recent years a few birds have remained for the winter. In Britain in the last twenty-five years Lesser Black-backed Gulls have increased greatly as wintering birds with over 7,000 now regularly staying behind.

Lesser Black-backs return to their colonies in March and commence laying at the end of April. The nests are quite bulky and are constructed of dried vegetation from the surrounding areas. They are usually built on fairly flat ground, and often among Herring Gull nests. On the Saltee Islands the favourite

Numbers have declined by half in the early 1980s due to botulism.

118

Top – The Great Black-backed Gull nests on the highest parts of the Saltee Islands, often out in the open on the flat summits. Its large size and massive bill enable it to kill and eat other seabirds and their remains can often be found close to the gulls' nests.

Middle – The Lesser Black-backed Gull is less predatory than its larger relative. This bird is still sitting on unhatched eggs while the day-old chick huddles close to its parent for protection and warmth.

Left – This hungery Herring Gull chick is waiting for its parent to regurgitate half-digested food which it has brought back to the nest-site.

habitat is the bracken choked fields away from the more precipitous parts of the islands. The normal clutch is three eggs but sometimes four are found, and they can often vary greatly in ground colouring and markings. They are smaller and usually darker than those of the Great Black-back, but cannot usually be distinguished from those of the Herring Gull. The eggs are incubated in turn by both parents and hatch after about four weeks. It takes a further seven weeks for the young to fledge and then they usually stay in the vicinity of the colony for a couple of months before migrating south.

The Saltee Islands and the Blasket Islands (in Kerry) house the largest Lesser Black-backed Gull colonies in Ireland, but at the Saltees the numbers fluctuate quite considerably. Peak numbers of about 550 pairs were recorded in the mid-1960s, the majority on Great Saltee, but in 1975 less than 200 pairs bred on Great Saltee and about 150 pairs were on Little Saltee and the decline has continued. In Ireland generally there has been a marked increase in recent decades, but even so a total of only 1,700 breeding pairs was recorded around the Irish coast in a survey carried out in 1969 and 1970. However, the overall total for Ireland is greater than this as some birds also nest on islands in some of the larger lakes in the west. Compared with Britain the Irish population is tiny: in 1969 and 1970 nearly 47,000 pairs were counted at British coastal colonies, 17,500 at Walney Island (Lancashire) alone.

Outside the British Isles the Lesser Black-backed Gull is found breeding in Iceland, the Faeroes, north-west France, Holland, Denmark, all round the Baltic Sea, and northwards along the Norwegian coast to north-west Russia. Two distinct sub-species occur within this range: in the eastern part the birds have much darker wings and mantles and look much more like small Great Black-backs, but with yellow legs.

8. The Herring Gull – *Larus argentatus*
This species is one of the most numerous, adaptable and best-known of the gulls, occurring both on the coast and inland in large numbers, and often frequenting cities and towns. In appearance the adults are white on the head, body and tail and have pale grey wings and mantles, with black and white wing tips. The bill is yellow with a red spot on the tip of the lower mandible, the eye is pale yellow, and the legs and feet are fleshy pink. In winter the adult birds have pale brownish flecks on the head. Young birds attain their adult plumage in their fourth year: in their first year they are very like young Lesser Black-backs, but they gradually get the pale grey on the wings and mantle. In size Herring Gulls are a little bigger than Lesser Black-backs, and are more fierce looking – but they are considerably smaller than the Great Black-back. The calls of the Herring Gull are very variable but are well-known to most people.

Herring Gulls breed in large colonies all round the coasts of Ireland. They breed not only on steep cliffs, stacks and grassy slopes on islands and head-lands, but also on salt-marshes, sand-dunes, and some nest on lake-islands some distance from the sea. In recent years they have even taken to nesting on roof-tops and chimney stacks in towns. On the Saltee Islands the birds nest on the boulder cliffs and the slopes leading down to them, as well as in "inland" sites on flat ground among bracken. In recent years they have taken to building in large numbers on the boulder beach on the north side of Great Saltee, possibly driven there by human disturbance at their more accessible sites. The breeding cycle is very similar to that of the Lesser Black-back, in terms of nest building, egg laying, clutch size, incubation and fledging periods, and the actual nests, eggs and downy young are hardly distinguishable from those of the Lesser Black-backs. However, the Herring Gulls are far more numerous and widespread on the islands; in the 1970s there were over 7,000 pairs, about 5,000 of which were on Great Saltee. The numbers have increased greatly since the 1950s but are now declining due to botulism. This increase fitted in with the general trend elsewhere and was probably due to the adaptability of the species in seeking out new food sources and the fact that large numbers can find ample food throughout the year at rubbish tips, sewage outfalls, abattoirs and other scavenging places — and of course large numbers will also follow fishing fleets for the offal thrown overboard, and on farmland will eat worms and grubs turned up by the plough.

Herring Gulls are rather sedentary birds and when the breeding colonies are vacated in late summer the birds usually make for the nearest towns, harbours and estuaries where they can scavenge for food. In the past they probably dispersed around the coasts and fed mainly on shellfish and marine worms, but now the biggest concentrations are found living off the wastes produced by human populations. A feature of the great increase in Herring Gull numbers has been the increasing tendency for flocks to move far inland in search of food, especially in winter.

A survey in 1969 and 1970 showed that the total Irish breeding population of Herring Gulls was about 52,000 pairs. This compares with a total of about 280,000 pairs in Britain of which over half were in Scotland. Outside the British Isles the Herring Gull is found throughout the northern hemisphere and is separated into about ten sub-species which are distinguished mainly by differing shades of grey on the wings, and some sub-species also have yellowish legs. In Eurasia birds breed from Iceland east to the Bering Sea, north to about 78° and south to about 30°. In North America the species breeds from Alaska south-east to the Great Lakes and the Gulf of St. Lawrence, and then south to New York. The species is migratory in parts of its range and in winter birds are found in the Gambia, the Red Sea, north-west India, east China, and in Central America.

9. The Kittiwake — *Rissa tridactyla*

This small dainty gull, so called because of its "kittiwake"-sounding cry, belongs to a different *Genus* than the other three nesting gulls on the Saltees. It is probably the only true sea-gull as it comes ashore only at nesting time and never wanders inland like the other species: indeed, many Kittiwakes spend the entire winter far out on the ocean, as far west as the east coast of North America. The bird is only 16 inches from bill-tip to tail tip and has a buoyant flight and mild dove-like expression, not at all like the fierce expressions of the larger gulls. Like the other gulls it is basically white, with medium grey wings and mantle, intermediate in shade between a Herring Gull and a Lesser Black-back. The wing tips are completely black and look as if they have been carefully dipped into indian ink. The eye is dark, as are the legs and feet, while the bill is a greenish yellow, lacks a red spot and is fine by comparison with the heavy bills of the larger species. The birds are generally silent away from the breeding colonies but make loud squawking "kittiwake" cries as they circle about the cliff-face on the updraughts.

Immature Kittiwakes differ greatly from the immatures of the larger gulls, totally lacking the brown spotted plumage. Instead they are a mixture of white, grey and black. The black is mainly on the back of the neck, the tip of the tail, and it forms an "M"-shaped mark across the wings. The rest of the wings and the back are grey. The immatures retain this plumage during their first year but thereafter, until they mature at three, they look like the adults apart from a grey mark at the back of the neck. They often spend their entire immature life away at sea.

The nest-site chosen by the Kittiwake is also very different from those of the larger gulls. They construct compact nests of grass and seaweed on tiny ledges on sheer cliffs of solid rock or boulder-clay, usually cementing the nesting materials together, and the whole structure to the cliff, with their own droppings. Often the nests are very tightly packed together and two or three nests sometimes touch. Breeding birds sometimes return to the colonies in January, but March is more normal. Nests are then repaired or constructed and egg-laying usually begins in late April or early May. Unlike the large gulls which lay three eggs, the Kittiwake's normal clutch is two and the eggs are relatively large and pale, with small spots. Incubation lasts about twenty five days and the newly-hatched chicks are covered in soft silver-grey down. Because of the precipitous nature of the colony site the young must remain in the nests until they are well able to fly and they have a strong self-preservatory instinct to cling to the small nests, facing in towards the cliff-face. It takes about six weeks for them to grow their feathers and learn to fly, and they disperse rapidly to sea after fledging.

Kittiwakes do not scavenge like other gulls but feed almost entirely on small fish, crustaceans and planktonic invertebrates, which they procure either by sitting on the water and catching their prey from the surface, or by plunge-diving for food under the surface. During the breeding season birds will often range up to forty miles out to sea from the colonies in search of food and they will fish both by day and by night. Food for the young is regurgitated by the adults when they return to the nests. In winter large flocks of Kittiwakes follow fishing boats and feed on offal thrown overboard.

On the Saltee Islands Kittiwakes are almost entirely confined to the larger island as the cliffs on Little Saltee are too low. In step with a general increase in the species in the British Isles in the last two or three decades the Great Saltee population has gone from less than 1,000 pairs thirty years ago to about 3,500 pairs now. The colonies range in size from just a few nests up to a couple of hundred and are distributed all along the cliffs at the southern side of the island.

In Ireland there are over 43,000 pairs of Kittiwakes and besides the Great Saltee colonies large numbers are found on the coasts of Waterford, Cork, Kerry, Clare, Galway, Mayo, Sligo, Donegal, Antrim and Dublin. In a survey carried out in 1969 and 1970 the grand total for the British Isles was found to exceed 470,000 pairs, making the Kittiwake one of the most abundant breeding seabird of the area. The species is extremely abundant in other parts of its North Atlantic range where it breeds primarily in the cold water areas of

Top — This Razorbill has just taken off, and is using its legs and tail to provide extra lift. This bird has to take off from a height because of its heavy body and is probably setting out to sea to catch small sprats.

Right — A Razorbill and its chick. The chick is just a few days old and still has the egg-tooth on the tip of its bill: a sharp encrustation which the bird uses to chip its way out of the shell. In a week or ten days the young bird will jump from its ledge to the sea below and, tended by its parents, continue its growth away from the islands.

Below — Kittiwakes build their nests close together on narrow ledges on sheer cliffs. This group shows three stages of development — the egg, weak newly-hatched chicks and a young bird beginning to grow its feathers.

the Arctic and sub-Arctic. Colonies extend from the Gulf of St. Lawrence to Baffin Island in Canada, to Greenland, Iceland, the Faeroes, and the coast of Norway north-eastwards to the north coast of Russia and islands in the Arctic Ocean. There are small numbers too in Brittany and Denmark. The Atlantic Kittiwake is replaced by a different sub-species in the North Pacific.

10. The Razorbill — *Alca torda*

Next to the Guillemot Razorbills are the most numerous cliff-nesting seabirds on the Saltee Islands. They are rather smaller than the Guillemot and are squatter looking. The head and upper-parts are black and the under-parts are gleaming white. The birds' bills are very distinctive, being heavy, laterally compressed and slightly hooked. There is a white vertical line in the middle, and a thin white line runs from the base of the bill to the brown eye. When the bill is opened it reveals a bright yellow inside. Razorbills have short small wings which they flap rapidly in flight, but when taking off from the cliff birds often swoop towards the water using a peculiar slow-motion flap, until they have gained sufficient air-speed to adopt their fast level flight. In calm conditions they often experience some difficulty taking off from the water and have to patter across the surface for some distance before getting airborne. On cliff ledges or boulders Razorbills stand upright like penguins and waddle rather clumsily about maintaining their balance with the help of their stiff pointed tails. Large numbers of Razorbills often gather on the sea below the nesting cliffs, strung out in long rafts. They often dive simultaneously and may co-operate in "rounding up" shoals of small fish. When feeding their young they are able to hold several fish together in their bills, secured cross-wise on back-facing barbs inside the bill. They are expert divers and propel themselves under water with both their wings and webbed feet.

Razorbill colonies are usually less densely packed than those of Guillemots, and the birds usually lay their solitary egg under cover of a boulder or in a crevice. No nest is made: the female simply deposits her egg on the bare earth or rock. The egg is chalky white in colour and is heavily spotted and blotched with black, especially at the more rounded end. Birds return to the colonies in January or February, but often the birds return to sea for several days between visits to the cliffs. As the laying period approaches the visits are more frequent and prolonged until egg-laying takes place at the end of April or in early May. The egg is incubated for 34 to 39 days and the newly hatched chick has dark brown down on the body and pale grey on the head. This down is soon lost and replaced by feathers and at two weeks of age the chicks look like miniature adults but with disproportionally large legs and feet, and small bills. When only about half grown at eighteen days the chick makes its way to the cliff-edge, encouraged by one of the parents, and then jumps and flutters down to the sea on its tiny wings. It is accompanied on the sea by one or both of its parents and quickly moves away from the colony. As the chick continues its growth on the sea it is fed by its parents until able to fend for itself.

On the Saltee Islands Razorbills can be found in large numbers all along the cliffs on the southern side of the Great Saltee, and also on a section of the south side of the small island. Most of the birds on Great Saltee nest under large lichen-covered boulders below the cliff top, but at the southern end of the island many are found nesting among the scattered boulders on the Sea Campion covered slopes high above the cliff top. Because of the concealed nest sites it is difficult to make an accurate census of the Razorbill population but it is believed that about 10,000 pairs nested in the early 1960s. Nowadays less than half that number breeds on Great Saltee, but in fact numbers have actually increased since the population was severely reduced by losses in the "Torrey Canyon" oil spill off Cornwall, and by a mysterious large-scale "kill" in the Irish sea area in autumn 1969. About 200 pairs breed on Little Saltee.

In autumn Razorbills from Irish and west British colonies move south to the Bay of Biscay, down the west coast of Iberia, and often into the Mediterranean. Some also move east up the English Channel to the southern North Sea. Many of the Scottish Razorbills, on the other hand, move eastwards to the coasts of southern Scandinavia. Elsewhere Razorbills are found on the west side of the North Atlantic from west Greenland to Labrador and south to Maine, and on the east side from north-west Russia south to Brittany, including parts of the Baltic: they also breed in Iceland.

11. The Guillemot — *Uria aalge*

The Guillemot is larger than the Razorbill, though slimmer and longer necked. Its bill is long and dagger-shaped. In colour the species has uniform dark brown plumage on the head, neck and upper surfaces of the body, while the underparts are pure white. The legs and bill are blackish and the latter has a yellow-orange inside. Some birds have a distinct white ring around the eyes with a tapering white streak running backwards from this ring: such birds are known as "bridled" Guillemots, and the proportion of "bridled" birds increases in the northerly populations of Guillemots. Like the Razorbill the Guillemot has small wings and legs set far back in the body and they too have the upright penguin-like stance when perched on ledges and rocks. In winter much of the Guillemot's face becomes white but a dark brown streak extends through this white area from the eye.

When not on their breeding sites Guillemots spend most of their time on the sea, swimming about and diving for small fish such as sand eels and sprats. They use both their wings and legs underwater and can remain submerged for over a minute. When moving from one feeding area to another groups of Guillemots fly low in line with whirring wings. As they come in to land on their nesting ledges they use their spread webbed feet as rudders and brakes before dropping awkwardly onto the rocks. When feeding young they usually bring in only one medium-sized fish held lengthwise in the bill, unlike the Razorbills and Puffins which bring several small fish held crosswise.

Guillemots visit their breeding colonies in mid-winter, usually only for short periods in the morning, but as laying time approaches visits are more prolonged and frequent. They make no nest but simply deposit their single pear-shaped egg on the bare rock. There is a general mess of guano on the nesting ledges and this helps to "stick" the egg to its precarious site and should it move or roll in spite of this its shape often causes it to spin in position rather than topple over the edge. Where nesting space is limited and where the colonies are large and dense the eggs can be strewn about in great numbers with just a few inches between them. This congestion gives rise to much squabbling among the incubating adults and their neighbours and dense colonies of Guillemots are very noisy places with a cacophony of rising and falling "murring" sounds echoing around the cliffs. The eggs themselves vary greatly in colour; almost all are heavily blotched with black and brown spots, but the ground colour can be pale brown, chalky white, or various shades of blue and green. Most are laid at the end of April or during the first half of May and hatch after 32 to 34 days of incubation. Losses of eggs are heavy, especially where colonies are subject to human disturbance — as large numbers of birds are scared off the ledges some eggs inevitably roll off and are broken; others are taken by gulls while unattended by the parent Guillemots. The newly-hatched Guillemot chick has sooty black down on the upperparts and white down underneath. The black down has a characteristic spikey appearance and the tips of these spikes are pale. When the chicks are about a third grown three weeks or so from hatching the down is completely replaced by feathers and they look like miniature versions of their parents. When excitedly awaiting a meal, or when frightened by aggressive neighbours the more advanced chicks make an incredibly piercing and loud continuous peeping call. When ready to leave the ledges the young are encouraged by the parents to leap and parachute down to the water, with fluttering wings and spread legs to slow their fall. The departure from the colony usually takes place late in the evening and the young birds swim away to sea with their parents. While their growth continues at sea and they perfect their fishing technique the young Guillemots are tended by their parents, so it is a common sight to see parties of three Guillemots at sea in July and August: two adults and one smaller bird, the chick. Because of their habit of returning to the colonies in November and December Guillemots usually do not wander great distances from their natal areas, though birds from Irish colonies are sometimes found in winter on the west coast of France and in north Spain: birds from Scottish colonies occasionally occur on the coasts of Norway and Denmark.

On the Saltee Islands Guillemots are confined to the larger island: the cliffs on Little Saltee are simply not high enough or sheer enough for this species. On Great Saltee dense colonies are found almost the whole way along the southern side of the island, mostly on open ledges, but also among clusters of boulders below the cliff-tops. Guillemots have always been the most numerous breeding auks on Great Saltee but in recent decades their fortunes have varied considerably. In the early 1960s the population was estimated at about 15,000 pairs but numbers had fallen to under 10,000 pairs by 1969. Then in September 1969 thousands of Guillemots died in the Irish sea area, possibly due to a combination of bad weather, shortage of food, marine pollution and other factors, and the following summer the Great Saltee population was down to less than 5,000 pairs. However, since then numbers have built up again and currently stand at about 15,000 pairs. Hopefully this trend will continue.

Elsewhere in Ireland Guillemots are found in about fifty sites. The largest colonies are on Rathlin Island, Co. Antrim and there are other very large colonies in Counties Donegal, Clare, Cork and Dublin, and smaller ones in Counties Sligo, Mayo, Galway, Kerry and Waterford. The total Irish population is probably over 80,000 breeding pairs, while Britain has about half a million

126

Above – A fine mass of Guillemots at their nest sites on a treacherous boulder-clay cliff. Photographs such as this are often used to census large gathering of breeding seabirds: in this one there are 346 Guillemots visible, and also five Razorbills and a Shag. The problem is to determine how many breeding pairs 346 birds represent!

Below – A mass of Guillemots perch on a flat rock. They can easily be distinguished from the Razorbills by their dagger-shaped bills, larger size and browner heads and backs.

pairs, most of which are concentrated in northern Scotland.

Guillemots are found in both the North Atlantic and the North Pacific. In the western North Atlantic the range embraces Newfoundland, the Gulf of St. Lawrence and parts of Labrador, as well as a small part of sub-Arctic Greenland. In the east they are found in Iceland and Arctic islands as far east as Novaya Zemlya, and south to the Faeroes, islands in the Baltic, north-west France, and the Berlengas off western Iberia. In the Pacific Guillemots are found on both sides, from Japan through islands in the Bering Sea to Alaska and south to Oregon.

12. The Puffin — *Fratercula arctica*

This is the smallest and most colourful of the three auks breeding on the Saltee Islands, and they are rather comical little birds in both appearance and behaviour. Like the other auks they are basically black and white, but their bills, eyes and feet are an incongruous mixture of colours. The large laterally flattened triangular bill is banded vertically in red, yellow and blue and is separated from the face by a fleshy yellow rosette at each side of the "mouth". The dark eye is surrounded by a red ring and small triangles of bluish skin. In winter the Puffin loses these eye and "mouth" adornments and also parts of its bill, so that it is a much duller and smaller-billed bird for part of the year. However, its legs and feet remain a bright orange throughout the year. The bird has greyish-white cheeks which are separated from the pure white of the underparts by a black neck. Immature birds look like adults in winter but have even smaller bills and these are dark grey in colour.

Puffins usually nest in large colonies on steep slopes covered with short grasses, sea campion or thrift. They excavate their own nest burrows and when this operation is in progress showers of earth can be seen coming out of the holes. Sometimes they will share a burrow entrance with rabbits or Manx Shearwaters. In some colonies the Puffins nest mainly in holes and crevices in boulder scree, or in burrows in small deposits of earth on ledges quite low down on the cliffs. The birds return to the area of their colonies between mid-March and early April and gather on the sea for several days before venturing onto the slopes. After two or three false starts the birds remain on land and begin nesting activities. When the burrows have been excavated a few pieces of dried vegetation are usually taken into the nesting chamber at the end and then the females lay their single white eggs, usually at the end of April. Incubation, shared by both parents, lasts about six weeks — much longer than in the other auks on the Saltees. The chick is covered with dark grey down and is fed on small fish which the parents bring in to the nesting chamber and leave on the floor. When the young bird is about six weeks old it is deserted by the parents and after a week of starvation it comes to the burrow entrance, falters awhile, and then at dusk leaves for the sea. As the young fledge the colonies are rapidly deserted and by mid-August few Puffins remain on land. They spend the seven winter months out at sea and little is known about their lives during this period. Birds from British and Irish colonies appear to resort to the North Sea and the Atlantic coasts of Europe as far south as Morocco, and also the western Mediterranean. There are a couple of records of Puffins ringed in western Scotland being recovered off Newfoundland and it may be that some numbers move far out into the Atlantic for the winter.

Puffins breed on both Saltee Islands. Because of their habit of nesting under-ground they are notoriously difficult to census, but current estimates suggest that there are probably not much more than a thousand pairs, the vast majority of which are on Great Saltee. Undoubtedly numbers were much greater in the past — photographs taken between 1910 and 1913 show large numbers on slopes now practically deserted — and human disturbance and increases in the numbers of predatory gulls may be among the main causes of the decline. Those now nesting on the islands are confined largely to the less accessible parts of the southern side of the large island and hopefully they will at least hold their own from now on.

There are only twenty to twenty-five Puffin colonies around the Irish coast, and of these only six or seven hold more than 1,000 pairs. The largest concentrations are in Kerry, Mayo and Donegal: Puffin Island, Great Skellig and Inishtearaght (Co. Kerry), Illaunmaistir (Co. Mayo), and mainland cliffs in Donegal in the Tormore, Horn Head and Malin Head areas, are among the most important areas. In Britain the main concentrations are in the Hebrides, Ornkeys and Shetland, and on the mainland cliffs of north and east Scotland and on the north-east coast and islands of England. There is also a large concentration on the south-west Welsh islands.

The Puffin, separated into two sub-species — large-billed Arctic and small-billed southern birds — breed on both sides of the Atlantic and on adjacent Arctic islands. They are found in Labrador, New Brunswick and south to Maine, on both the west and east coasts of Greenland, in Iceland, the Faeroes, Bear Island, Jan Mayen, Spitzbergen, Novaya Zemlya, the north-west European coast from the Kola Peninsula to southern Norway, on islands in the entrance to the Baltic, in Britain and Ireland, and on the Channel Islands and the coast of Brittany.

Puffins usually return to their nesting burrows with a beak-full of small sprats which they catch one at a time and hold in their bills by means of small interior barbs. Collecting fish this way saves the birds from having to make many journeys between the nesting site and the feeding grounds.

Chapter 13
The Other Breeding Birds

A perusal of the list of the birds of the Saltee Islands (page 144) reveals that fifty species breed or have bred on the islands and two others are possible breeders. The twelve breeding seabirds have already been dealt with at some length and in this chapter the remaining forty are discussed. When one leaves aside the seabirds the remaining species are inevitably almost all land-birds: three exceptions are swimming birds, the Mallard, Red-breasted Merganser and Shelduck – and there are four others which are not true land-birds, the Oyster-catcher, Lapwing, Ringed Plover and Snipe. If you consider the size of the islands – Great Saltee is 219 acres, Little Saltee 98 acres – their remoteness from the nearest part of the mainland, their exposure to the prevailing south-west winds, and their general lack of tall vegetation, the diversity of breeding birds is remarkable. Even if these forty species are in themselves mostly "common or garden" birds the fact that they manage, or have managed to breed on the islands in such diversity is of great interest to ornithologists. The fact that they are present on the islands during the summer months at the same time as the breeding seabirds means that visitors to the islands can see these species too, if they keep an eye open for them as they make their way to and from the seabird cliffs.

Because Little Saltee is so seldom visited, compared to Great Saltee, our knowledge of its breeding birds is very sketchy and no doubt more species will be found breeding there in future. In fact at present only thirteen species, other than the seabirds, have been proved to breed on Little Saltee, and two of these, the Peregrine and Swallow, have not bred for many years. The eleven which breed, or have bred within the last few years, are the Mallard, Shelduck, Oyster-catcher, Rock Dove, Skylark, Hooded Crow, Blackbird, Stonechat, Meadow Pipit, Rock Pipit, and Starling. Although this list is probably not complete, due to lack of observations, it is unlikely that Little Saltee will ever rival Great Saltee in breeding bird diversity: although considerably closer to the mainland, its small size and restricted habitats militate against bird diversity.

Great Saltee, on the other hand, has been visited on countless occasions since the end of the last century, and while the main objective of most of the early visitors was to see and study the seabirds, a number of them also noted the other species present on the island. For example, T. H. Mason writing in *The Islands of Ireland* in 1936 listed twenty-three non-seabird species and indicated that he himself had found seventeen of these breeding. When Saltee Bird Observatory was established on Great Saltee in spring 1950 its main objective was the study of bird migration in spring and autumn, but during the fourteen years of the Observatory's operation much information was also gathered on the breeding birds. A paper by R. F. Ruttledge entitled *Migrant and other Birds of Great Saltee, Co. Wexford* published in 1963 shortly after the Bird Observatory was closed, recorded twenty-six non-seabird breeders. Then in the years 1968 to 1972, during the course of field-work for *The Atlas of Breeding Birds of Britain and Ireland* a number of visits were made to Great Saltee specifically to record all breeding species, both seabirds and land-birds. This survey added a number of species to the island's list, notably the Pheasant (introduced since 1963), Wood Pigeon, Cuckoo, Song Thrush, Grasshopper Warbler, Starling and Yellowhammer. Further work since 1972, notably by K. W. Perry for his book (with S. W. Warburton) *The Birds and Flowers of the Saltee Islands,* and by the present writer, and some researching of the literature have brought the species list to its present level of thirty-eight/forty (plus twelve seabirds). The two "doubtfuls" are the Magpie, recorded by T. H. Mason as breeding (prior to 1936), but an extremely rare visitor to the island since at least 1950; and the Partridge, recorded by Mason as present on the island prior to 1936 and reintroduced in the 1960s, but not yet proved to have bred successfully.

Regrettably, a number of species have ceased to breed. Particularly sad is the departure of the Peregrine. This magnificent bird-of-prey nested on Great Saltee from at least the end of the last century until the late 1940s, and then on Little Saltee until 1955. It was much persecuted by egg-collectors and by falconers taking young birds to train, but may have finally succumbed to environmental pollution. Another sad loss is that of the Corncrake. This species probably last nested about the turn of the century but then ceased to do so long before the general decline of the species in Britain and Ireland which was caused by modern farming methods. Other species which have ceased to breed on Great Saltee are the Swallow (due to renovations of the old buildings), Rook (recorded as nesting in 1929 but not since), Pied Wagtail (probably has not nested within the last thirty years), and Yellowhammer (as mentioned above, recorded in 1968-72, once in 1968, but not since).

The thirty-two species which breed regularly, or which have bred in recent years, are mostly quite common birds on the mainland. The only ones which can be regarded as scarce in south-east Ireland are the Chough, Raven and Red-breasted Merganser. In the case of the Cough Great Saltee is the most easterly outpost of the species on the south coast of Ireland, and none is found right along the east coast until one reaches the cliffs of Antrim in Northern Ireland. Up to five or six pairs of these handsome black birds with red legs and bill nested on Great Saltee in the early 1930s. Then the species was absent as a breeder for many years, but in the last few years a pair has bred successfully on the island.

The populations of the other species are small. The table on page 133 divides

Below – *Twenty-five to thirty pairs of Blackbirds breed on Great Saltee, a few on Little Saltee. In October and November many hundreds of migrants from Britain and the Continent rest on the islands before continuing to wintering grounds in Ireland.*

Right – *A Sedge Warbler sings wheezily to proclaim its breeding territory in a bramble patch on Great Saltee. This species, a summer visitor from Africa, is one of the most noticeable of the breeding song-birds of the islands.*

Bottom – *Lapwings nest in a couple of damp short-grass areas on Great Saltee and seem to spend much of their time mobbing gulls which fly over the breeding areas.*

them into two groups those with regular population of under ten breeding pairs, and those with populations of ten to thirty breeding pairs.

1 - 9 breeding pairs	*10 - 30 breeding pairs*
Mallard	Pheasant
Shelduck	Rock Dove
Oystercatcher	Jackdaw
Lapwing	Blackbird
Ringed Plover	Sedge Warbler
Snipe	Dunnock
Wood Pigeon	Rock Pipit
Cuckoo	
Skylark	
Hooded Crow	
Wren	
Song Thrush	
Wheatear	
Stonechat	
Robin	
Grasshopper Warbler	
Whitethroat	
Spotted Flycatcher	
Meadow Pipit	
Starling	
Linnet	
Reed Bunting	

Not all the breeding birds of the Saltees are resident throughout the year. In fact eight are purely summer visitors, not only to the islands but to Ireland generally. The Corncrake and Swallow are included in this category and although they no longer breed on the islands they still occur as passage migrants in spring and autumn — the latter species in considerable numbers. The other summer visitors are the Cuckoo, Wheatear, Grasshopper Warbler, Sedge Warbler, Whitethroat, and Spotted Flycatcher. Some of these birds which breed on the islands are probably just migrants which happen to chance on the islands on their migration north in spring, and having found conditions to be suitable they decide to stay and breed. But others return year after year from wintering grounds in Africa, and their young in turn also come back to the Saltees. This traditional attachment to the islands is particularly marked in the Sedge Warbler: a number of ringed individuals have been retrapped on Great Saltee one or more breeding seasons after they were first caught. It is quite probable that some breeding species, or at least a proportion of their breeding population, also leave the islands to spend the winter on the main-land: a number of birds ringed as nestlings or breeding adults have been recovered on the mainland in the following or subsequent winters. Perhaps the islands are too inhospitable in winter and the birds have to seek more sheltered areas elsewhere.

In spite of the islands' small size and marine environment they do have quite

Above – A few pairs of Oystercatchers nest on the Saltees, both on the boulder beaches and in the fields. This bird is uttering its piping alarm note to attract the intruder away from the nest.

Below left – A family of Choughs play in the updraughts along the cliffs of Great Saltee. Forty years ago several pairs nested on the island but nowadays only one or two do so. The species is rare in the east of Ireland but becomes progressively more numerous along the Waterford and Cork coasts.

Below right – Rock Pipits are common residents on the Saltees and are often seen at the Great Saltee landing place feeding on flies on the piles of rotting seaweed. They are extremely sedentary and few even venture the short distance to the mainland.

a wide range of habitat types — especially Great Saltee — and no doubt this accounts to a large extent for the great variety of breeding birds. Mallard are not very fussy about where they nest, so long as there is plenty of thick ground cover to conceal the nest and eggs and the sitting female, and there is plenty of cover among the bracken and brambles of the Saltees. The lack of a fresh-water pond of any consequence does not seem to be a deterrent. The Red-breasted Merganser and Shelduck like dense ground cover too and they are quite happy to have the sea nearby. The Peregrine, when it nested on the islands, had inaccessible cliff ledges on which to nest, and a plentiful supply of food, in the form of hapless seabirds. The introduced Pheasant appears to be doing surprisingly well: again the thick bracken and brambles seem to provide them with the cover, shelter and food they require. The Oystercatchers and Ringed Plover utilise the small areas of shingle and sand, especially in the vicinity of the landing place and The Ring, and the former species also nests in the open short grass fields on The Waist of the island. Snipe and Lapwing usually nest in the rather damp grassy and rushy areas near the spring south of The Throne, and also in a field near The Ring. Rock Doves, as their name implies, nest in fissures and crevices, and they have a wide choice of these along the seaward side of the island, and they probably compete for the best sites with Jackdaws and Razorbills. The Wood Pigeon, which is a newcomer to Great Saltee, was first found nesting on the ground under bracken — a most unusual site — and birds still do so, though one or two pairs have recently used more conventional sites in trees and bushes, especially in the garden behind the old house. Hooded Crows also use the garden trees, though a pair on Little Saltee have nested on the ruined building. Other species which share the cliffs with the Rock Doves, Jackdaws and the thousands of seabirds are the Raven and Chough. Starlings nest in the old buildings and so too did the Pied Wagtails and Swallows in the past, while the Rock Pipits usually nest down by the boulder beaches where they are close to the swarms of flies that infest the banks of rotting seaweed. All the other song-birds nest either among the dense bracken and bramble, or in the sycamores, hawthorn and Olearia of the garden or the few isolated willows, elders and other stunted trees scattered around The Waist of Great Saltee.

So, those species which are adaptable and can breed successfully in the abundant ground cover are limited in numbers not by lack of suitable habitat but by the overall size of the islands and the birds' own territorial requirements. Those which have more specialised nesting site requirements, such as the tree- and building-nesters, are limited by the acute shortage of these on the Saltees — but it is interesting that what few sites there are on the islands are occupied by the same species one might expect to find in similar sites on the mainland. In other words the isolation of the islands has not deterred these species from colonising them.

135

Chapter 14
Bird Migration

People interested in wildlife never cease to be fascinated by the extraordinary journeys which migratory birds undertake each spring and autumn as they travel between their traditional breeding grounds and their wintering areas. Small song-birds like Swallows, weighing less than an ounce, fly thousands of miles from Britain and Ireland to their wintering grounds in southern Africa, and they can accomplish this journey in just a few weeks. Manx Shearwaters, which nest in burrows on Great Saltee and on other islands around the British and Irish coasts, fly south-westwards across the Atlantic Ocean to spend the winter in the waters off the east coast of Brazil. Brent Geese which breed on high Arctic tundra on islands in Canada as far west as 105° west of Greenwich fly each autumn eastwards across the polar basin to Greenland and thence south-eastwards to the muddy bays and estuaries of the Irish coast. These are just three examples of migratory movements which are commonplace among birds: there are many other examples at least as interesting and spectacular, but it is not the purpose of this chapter to go into detail on the global wanderings of migratory birds. Rather is it intended to highlight the important role which the Saltee Islands play in assisting these birds on their way.

Bird migration has been a cause of great wonder and mystery for thousands of years. Peoples of past ages observed the comings and goings of the birds with the changing seasons and wondered how and why these events took place. Some interesting theories were put forward which, in the light of knowledge gained in the last hundred years or so, now appear incredible or absurd. For example as recently as two or three hundred years ago people thought Swallows went to the moon, or that they dived beneath the surface of ponds and cocooned themselves in mud at the bottom, there to spend the winter in hibernation. In Ireland long ago people observing the absence of Barnacle Geese from May to September (when they were in fact breeding in north-east Greenland) believed the birds were the final stage of a metamorphosis from shellfish. Believing this they argued that the geese were in fact fish and could therefore be eaten on Fridays: a messenger had to be sent from Rome to put them right and forbid the eating of Barnacle Geese on Fridays.

Myths like these persisted right up to the end of the last century — indeed, some peculiar ones persist to this day — but then naturalists began to understand the true nature and extent of bird migration. One of the most important innovations in the field of migration studies in the early days was the use of metal rings placed on the legs of captured birds which were then released to continue their journeys. The rings bore an address and a serial number and the ringer made a note, before each bird was released, of the number attached to each individual, and of course the name of the species and details of the place and date of release. A small percentage of these ringed birds were subsequently found elsewhere and the finder reported the fact to the address on the ring. By matching the finding details with the original ringing details it was possible to determine how far the bird had gone, how long it had taken on its journey, and so on. Over the years a series of recoveries of ringed birds would show up the migration route as well as the eventual destination, and other interesting information about a species' life-cycle. Bird ringing is still one of the most important means of piecing together the patterns of migration of the many birds which do migrate, and much work of this kind has been carried out at Great Saltee. In 1950 a Bird Observatory was established on the island and each spring and autumn, during the main migration periods, parties of ornithologists took it in turn to man the Observatory to record the daily movements of birds using the island as a stepping stone on their migrations, and many of these birds were trapped, ringed and released. Some were subsequently found in places as diverse as Russia, Norway, Libya and Spain. Saltee Bird Observatory operated until the spring of 1963 and during the fourteen years of study at Great Saltee much was learnt about the movements of birds in and out of and through Ireland, and a number of species not previously recorded in this country were observed on Great Saltee and added to the Irish List. Also, a number of species which had previously been considered very rare vagrants in Ireland were found to be regular passage migrants, albeit usually in small numbers. Since 1963 a few expeditions to the island have been organised in spring and autumn and ringing of migratory birds is continuing on a less formal basis than when the Bird Observatory was in operation. On the other hand much more ringing of the breeding seabirds has been carried out in the last ten years or so, with up to 5,000 birds (mainly nestlings) being ringed each year. The result of this is that we now know a great deal more about where our breeding seabirds spend the winter months, and we also know, from the circumstances surrounding the recoveries, what threats and dangers they face while away at sea — for example, many Razorbills and Guillemots ringed on the Saltee Islands are found covered in oil, or drowned in fishing nets.

Seabirds, mainly Cormorants, are ringed each year on Little Saltee, but it seems no-one has ever stayed on the island in spring or autumn to study the great migratory movements of small song-birds and others. However, it is very unlikely that Little Saltee is anything like as important as Great Saltee as a resting place for these migrants. It is neither the first land-fall for tired birds arriving from the south in spring, nor the last jumping-off point for birds setting off for Cornwall, France or Spain in autumn. Also its small size and less

Top – The Willow Warbler,
one of the daintiest and most
melodious of the warblers is
a common spring and autumn
migrant on the Saltees.
Although only six or eight
grammes in weight this
species migrates from
Lapland to south of the
Sahara.

Right – A Sand Martin's
migration is temporarily
arrested by a mist-net. Note
that the bird is already bear-
ing a ring. Many thousands
of migrant and breeding birds
have been ringed on the
Saltee Islands.

Extreme right – In recent
years a pair of Starlings has
nested in a crevice in the old
farmhouse. In autumn the
species is a very common
migrant, with up to 10,000
being recorded in one day in
November.

attractive range of habitats would tend to deter migrants from using it when a much more suitable island is closeby. Great Saltee is undoubtedly the island to go to if you wish to see bird migration taking place. In spring the migration season usually extends from about the second or third week in March (though some of the birds which have spent the winter in Ireland have already moved east or north-east to Europe by then) until about the middle of May. However, stragglers continue to arrive from the south in the latter half of May, and even in early June, and sometimes much of the spring migration is held up by adverse weather conditions and many of the birds arrive a week or two later than usual. In autumn the southwards migration begins in mid-August with the departure of the Swifts and Cuckoos and the start of more protracted movements of other species. By the middle to end of October virtually all the summer visitors have moved away southwards, but it is then that the arrivals of the thrushes, finches and other birds which come to Ireland in large numbers for the winter really get under way, and these movements continue well into November. Then there are often hard-weather movements in December and January when large flocks of birds are forced by icy conditions on the Continent or in Britain to flee westwards to Ireland where the winter climate is usually less severe. So there are only very short periods during the year when migration of one sort or another is at a standstill.

Bird migration does in fact take many different forms and in Ireland the main types which occur include the arrivals in spring and departures in autumn of species which have spent the winter further south; the arrival in autumn and departure in spring of species which spend the winter here and breed further north; the passage through Ireland, or along its coasts of birds which neither breed here nor spend the winter here but simply use this country as a brief resting place on their journeys north in spring and south in autumn; the arrival in some winters of large numbers of birds fleeing from cold weather further east; the sometimes regular but more often sporadic invasions of species whose populations have reached a high level and which are forced to spread outside their normal range; the arrival of vagrants, sometimes many thousands of miles off course, blown by the winds to our shores; the departure and return of a proportion of the resident Irish birds which are known as partial migrants — and so on. All these forms of migration and bird movements can be observed at the Saltee Islands. Being situated in the south-east corner of Ireland they lie directly in the path of a great number of Irish summer visitors which leave the country each autumn.

The small land-birds are reluctant to set out across the sea and they tend to follow coastlines leading in the general direction of where they want to go, so streams of migrants move down the east coast of Ireland to Carnsore Point where they are joined by others which have arrived on the south coast and are moving along it in search of a short sea crossing. The migrants, still reluctant to set off out to sea, avail of the Saltees as a last foothold on land before launching off into the unknown. In spring, tired migrants on their return journey to Ireland, arrive in great numbers in the south-east and must welcome the Saltees as a landing place on which they can rest and feed and regain their strength. Small warblers, which may have flown non-stop from the north coast of Spain, land exhausted on Great Saltee having used up almost all their fat reserves and reduced their body weight to nearly 50% of normal. Resting and feeding on the island for a few days they can not only regain this lost weight but put on quite a bit extra which will enable them to fly another few hundred miles on the next leg of their journey, perhaps to Iceland or Scandinavia. In late autumn large flocks of thrushes, Starlings, finches and other wintering song-birds stream into Ireland from Europe. Again, birds coming from France or southern England find the Saltees a convenient resting place after their journey across the sea. Then there are the migrant seabirds which in autumn enter the Irish Sea at the north end as they follow the coast of Europe southwards. To get out of the Irish Sea to the open waters of the Atlantic many pass close around the "corner" at Carnsore Point and stream past the Saltees. These birds can be the common species familiar on the islands in summer, or they can be skuas from Arctic or sub-Arctic breeding grounds, or Great and Sooty Shear-waters from colonies in the southern hemisphere on *their* spring migration to breed in the Antipodean summer.

Vagrants, by definition, are birds which for one reason or another, have strayed far from their normal migration route. It may be they are young birds with an undeveloped sense of orientation that have simply gone the wrong way, or they may be birds which have encountered bad weather and have been blown off course. If migrating birds run into fog or heavy cloud cover and are unable to see the stars at night they become disoriented and tend to go along with the wind: if these winds are blowing from the east we can get vagrants from as far away as central Asia turning up on the Saltees — if there are strong westerlies then birds like White-rumped and Pectoral Sandpipers from North America can be swept across the Atlantic. In springtime it some-times happens that weather conditions are unusually favourable for migrants heading north from Africa to southern Europe. In such conditions some birds, such as the Night Heron, Alpine Swift, Red-rumped Swallow, Golden Oriole, Hoopoe and some of the southern European warblers "overshoot" their proper destinations and end up in south-east Ireland, often on the Saltee Islands.

The vast majority of migrants which occur on the Saltee Islands are either the regular summer and winter visitors which come to Ireland, or birds which breed in Greenland, Iceland, The Faeroes, Scotland, Scandinavia and northern Europe and which are on their way to wintering grounds in southern Europe or Africa. As already mentioned, some birds, mainly vagrants, wander from the North American continent, others from areas far to the east or south-east, such as Pallas's Grasshopper Warbler, the Barred Warbler, the Yellow-browed Warbler, Red-breasted Flycatcher, Rose-coloured Starling, Scarlet Rosefinch and Black-headed Bunting, to mention just a few of the small song-bird vagrants which have been seen on Great Saltee.

Most of the migrant seabirds and other waterbirds (the divers, grebes, wild-fowl and waders and so on) do not actually rest on the Saltees (though they do seek sheltered waters in the lee of the islands during storms), but rather pass by in the vicinity of the islands. The land-birds on the other hand do use the islands as a resting place, sometimes for just a few hours, more often for a couple of days, and occasionally for several weeks. Many of the small birds are night migrants, using the stars to navigate and resting and feeding during the day. It is not uncommon on Great Saltee, during the main migration periods,

Top — Only one or two pairs of Robins nest on Great Saltee, usually close to the old farmhouse. Up to a hundred migrants are occasionally recorded in autumn.

Middle — This Whitethroat, another African wintering warbler, has been netted and ringed on Great Saltee. Up to recently many hundreds of these birds could be seen on Great Saltee on spring migration, but the population has decreased greatly due to droughts in the wintering areas and the species is now found only in small numbers.

Left — Each spring, from mid-April to May, Cuckoos arrive from their wintering grounds in Africa and are frequently heard and seen on the Saltees. This bird has been caught by mist-net for ringing and release.

to rise in the morning and find the island "hopping" with small warblers, fly-catchers, Goldcrests and others which have arrived during the night and have landed to spend the day feeding before moving on again. Sometimes several thousand birds may be involved in these sudden arrivals, a phenomenon known to ornithologists as a "fall". Willow Warblers and Chiffchaffs are usually the species occurring most numerously in such "falls". Other species are purely day-time migrants: Swallows and martins are particularly so — they simply fly along with their mouths open and feed on aerial insects as they go. Meadow Pipits and Skylarks often migrate by day too, sometimes so high in the sky that they cannot be seen with the naked eye. On one occasion on Great Saltee, on a warm cloudless day in early September, there appeared to be no migration taking place. Then in the afternoon Meadow Pipits began to drop out of the clear blue sky in large numbers and descend to the water-hole in the centre of the island for a drink. Some nets were quickly erected in the area and in no time at all over one hundred birds were caught, ringed and let off again to continue their journey to France — a couple were actually recovered there later that autumn.

Kestrels occasionally wander to the islands from the mainland but they and other species of raptors are migrants too. The larger birds-of-prey, such as the Buzzard and the harriers can feed on the numerous rabbits and rats that inhabit the islands, as well as small birds. The Merlin and Sparrowhawk, which are bird-eating raptors, often migrate with smaller birds and feed from the flocks as they go. It is particularly noticeable that when large movements of Swallows and martins are in progress one or two Merlins are almost always in attendance: when hungry they swoop in and take a hapless bird for a meal.

To observe the seabird migrants it is best to take a comfortable position near the landing place or at Sebber, preferably at the top of the low boulder-clay cliff to get a view into the troughs of the swell, and with a pair of binoculars trained on the sea between the Great and Little Saltees watch for a while. It will soon become evident if there is a good passage of seabirds taking place: if you count the passing birds for, say, fifteen minutes and get more than a couple of dozen, then it is worth watching for a longer period — half an hour, an hour or even more. Inevitably, most of the birds will be the commoner species which nest on the islands (though the passing ones may well be from colonies hundreds of miles away), but the heavier the movement the more likely will it be that an unusual bird or two will be mixed with these. If shear-waters are taking part in the passage it is a good idea to watch out for Great, Sooty and Cory's Shearwaters mixed in with the Manx Shearwaters. Autumn is the best time for these as the first two species are by that time passing down the west coast of Europe on their great circular migration from breeding grounds in the southern hemisphere clockwise around the South and North Atlantic and back to the South Atlantic. The Great Shearwaters breed only on the Tristan da Cunha Islands in the South Atlantic, half-way between South America and the southern tip of Africa, yet many of these birds can be seen passing the Irish coast each autumn on their way back to their breeding grounds. Divers, mainly Great Northern and Red-throated, can also be seen passing, both in spring and autumn, and so too can Storm Petrels (and occasionally the rare Leach's Petrel), especially if a south-westerly gale has forced these oceanic birds close to the land. In such conditions in autumn look out for phalaropes bobbing about like corks on the rough sea. Although these tiny birds are waders they have lobed toes and are well able to swim: in fact they are much happier out on the oceans when they are away from their Arctic breeding places and they feed on tiny plankton floating on or near the surface. Skuas, too, can be seen passing, usually singly but sometimes in small groups, and as the Merlins follow the Swallows and martins the skuas often follow migrating terns or small gulls. They are parasitic birds and get much of their food by chasing the gulls and terns so persistently and expertly that the pursued birds are forced to disgorge their last meal: the skuas then give up the chase and drop to the water to eat the disgorged fish. The terns themselves are on their way in autumn from breeding grounds in Ireland and further north (right up to Spitzbergen and Greenland) to wintering grounds off the west coast of Africa. The Little Terns don't go futher south than the Tropic of Cancer, but the Roseate Terns go to the Gulf of Guinea, and the Sandwich Terns often as far south as Angola. The Arctic Tern, which is one of the most northerly breeding species, colonising areas in the middle 80° Latitude, is also probably the most southerly wintering species: some individuals have been seen fishing among the ice-floes of Antarctica in the southern summer. Some of the gulls also migrate, especially the Lesser Black-backed Gull which vacates its Irish breeding areas in autumn and sets off southwards to Spain and Portugal. The rarer gulls, such as the Glaucous (from Iceland), the Little (mainly from north-east Europe) and the Sabine's Gull (from the high Arctic and heading for south-west Africa) can sometimes be seen passing Great Saltee or dallying for a while on the island.

To date about sixty bird species which are rare in Ireland have been seen on the Saltee Islands and no doubt as observations continue more will be added to the islands' list. There are only about a dozen of the commoner Irish species which have not yet been seen on the islands — and some of these (for example the Red Grouse, Jay and Dipper) are unlikely to venture across the narrow strip of water separating the islands from the mainland — but so long as migratory birds, large and small, undertake journeys of thousands of miles between their summering and wintering quarters and are subject to the vagaries of the winds and weather they will continue to find in the Saltee Islands a welcome refuge where they can find food, rest and shelter.

This female Shelduck anxiously leads her brood of nine newly-hatched ducklings across open ground to the safety of the sea. Several pairs of these large handsome ducks breed on the Saltees.

Chapter 15
A List of Birds of the Saltee Islands

The following is a list of the 218 species which have been recorded on the Saltee Islands up to June 1977. They are arranged in the conventional systematic order as published by the British Trust for Ornithology in "A Species List of British and Irish Birds" (1971).

Key to Symbols

Breeding status —	B	= Breeds, or has bred in the 1970s.
	B?	= Possible breeder.
	PB	= Past breeder, before 1970.
General status —	V	= Vagrant, 1 - 10 records.
	R	= Rare, 11 - 50 records.
	S	= Scarce, usually less than 100 annually.
	C	= Common, usually more than 100 annually (and up to 20,000).

Species which appear in *italics* are rare in Ireland and need to be fully described for acceptance by the Irish Bird Records Panel and publication in the *Irish Bird Report*.

Species	Breeding Status	General Status	Species	Breeding Status	General Status
Black-throated Diver		V	Cormorant	B	C
Great Northern Diver		R/S	Shag	B	C
Red-throated Diver		S	Grey Heron		S
Great Crested Grebe		V	*Night Heron*		V
Red-necked Grebe		V	*Bittern*		V
Slavonian Grebe		V	Mallard	B	C
Little Grebe		V	Teal		C
Fulmar	B	C	Gadwall		V
Cory's Shearwater		V	Wigeon		S
Manx Shearwater	B	C	Shoveler		R/S
Great Shearwater		R/S	Scaup		R
Sooty Shearwater		S	Long-tailed Duck		V
Storm Petrel		S	*Velvet Scoter*		V
Leach's Petrel		V	Common Scoter		S
Gannet	B	C	Eider		V

Species	Breeding Status	General Status	Species	Breeding Status	General Status
Red-breasted Merganser	B	S	Ruff		V
Shelduck	B	C	Grey Phalarope		R
Greylag Goose		V	*Red-necked Phalarope*		V
White-fronted Goose		R	*Stone Curlew*		V
Snow Goose		V	Great Skua		S
Brent Goose		V	Pomarine Skua		R
Mute Swan		V	Arctic Skua		S
Whooper Swan		V	*Long-tailed Skua*		V
Buzzard		R	Great Black-backed Gull	B	C
Sparrowhawk		S	Lesser Black-backed Gull	B	C
Hen Harrier		R/S	Herring Gull	B	C
Montagu's Harrier		V	Common Gull		C
Peregrine	PB	S	Glaucous Gull		V
Merlin		S	Little Gull		V
Kestrel		S	Black-headed Gull		S
Partridge	B?	R	*Sabine's Gull*		V
Quail		R	Kittiwake	B	C
Pheasant	B	S/C	Black Tern		R
Water Rail		S	Common Tern		C
Corncrake	PB	S	Arctic Tern		C
Moorhen		V	Roseate Tern		C
Oystercatcher	B	C	Little Tern		S
Lapwing	B	C	Sandwich Tern		C
Ringed Plover	B	S	Razorbill	B	C
Grey Plover		S	Little Auk		V
Golden Plover		S	Guillemot	B	C
Dotterel		V	Black Guillemot		S
Turnstone		C	Puffin	B	C
Snipe	B	C	Stock Dove		V
Great Snipe		V	Rock Dove	B	C
Jack Snipe		S	Woodpigeon	B	C
Woodcock		S	Turtle Dove		S/C
Curlew		C	Collared Dove		V
Whimbrel		C	Cuckoo	B	S
Black-tailed Godwit		V	*Little Owl*		V
Bar-tailed Godwit		S	Long-eared Owl		V
Green Sandpiper		V	Short-eared Owl		R
Wood Sandpiper		V	Nightjar		S
Common Sandpiper		S	Swift		C
Redshank		S/C	*Alpine Swift*		V
Spotted Redshank		V	Kingfisher		V
Greenshank		S	Hoopoe		R
Knot		R/S	*Great Spotted Woodpecker*		V
Purple Sandpiper		S	*Wryneck*		V
Little Stint		V	*Short-toed Lark*		R
White-rumped Sandpiper		V	*Lesser Short-toed Lark*		V
Pectoral Sandpiper		V	*Woodlark*		V
Dunlin		S/C	Skylark	B	C
Curlew Sandpiper		V	Swallow	PB	C
Sanderling		S	*Red-rumped Swallow*		V

Species	Breeding Status	General Status	Species	Breeding Status	General Status
House Martin		C	Chiffchaff		C
Sand Martin		C	*Wood Warbler*		V
Golden Oriole		V	*Bonelli's Warbler*		V
Raven	B	S	*Yellow-browed Warbler*		V
Carrion/Hooded Crow	B[1]	R/S	Goldcrest		C
Rook	PB	S	*Firecrest*		V
Jackdaw	B	C	Spotted Flycatcher	B	C
Magpie		V	Pied Flycatcher		S
Chough	B	S	*Red-breasted Flycatcher*		R
Great Tit		R/S	Dunnock	B	C
Blue Tit		S	*Tawny Pipit*		V
Coal Tit		V	*Olive-backed Pipit*		V
Long-tailed Tit		V	Meadow Pipit	B	C
Treecreeper		V	*Tree Pipit*		S
Wren	B	S/C	*Red-throated Pipit*		V
Mistle Thrush		S	Rock/*Water Pipit*	B[2]	C/V
Fieldfare		C	Pied/White Wagtail	PB[3]	C
Song Thrush	B	C	Grey Wagtail		S
Redwing		C	Yellow/*Blue-headed Wagtail*		S/V
Ring Ouzel		S	Waxwing		V
Blackbird	B	C	*Woodchat Shrike*		R
Wheatear	B	C	*Lesser Grey Shrike*		V
Black-eared Wheatear		V	*Red-backed Shrike*		V
Stonechat	B	C	Starling	B	C
Stonechat	B	C	*Rose-coloured Starling*		V
Whinchat		S	Greenfinch		S/C
Redstart		S	Goldfinch		C
Black Redstart		S	Siskin		S/C
Nightingale		R	Linnet	B	C
Bluethroat		V	Twite		V
Robin	B	S/C	Redpoll		S
Rufous Bush Robin		V	Bullfinch		V
Grasshopper Warbler	B	S	*Scarlet Rosefinch*		V
Pallas's Grasshopper Warbler		V	Crossbill		V
Reed Warbler		V	Chaffinch		C
Sedge Warbler	B	C	Brambling		S
Aquatic Warbler		V	Corn Bunting		R
Melodious Warbler		R	Yellowhammer	PB	R
Icterine Warbler		V	*Black-headed Bunting*		V
Blackcap		S	*Red-headed Bunting*		V
Barred Warbler		V	*Ortolan Bunting*		R
Garden Warbler		S	*Little Bunting*		V
Whitethroat	B	C	Reed Bunting	B	S
Lesser Whitethroat		R	*Lapland Bunting*		R
Subalpine Warbler		V	Snow Bunting		R
Willow Warbler		C	House Sparrow		V
Greenish Warbler		V	Tree Sparrow		V

Notes: 1. The Hooded Crow is the form which breeds; the other is rare. 2. The Rock Pipit is the form which breeds; the other is vagrant. 3. The Pied Wagtail is the form which has bred; the other is a passage migrant.

A panoramic view from the Big Head, Great Saltee, looking north-eastwards over the bigger island, with the Little Saltee in the left background.

BREEDING SEABIRDS OF THE SALTEE ISLANDS
Estimated numbers of breeding pairs in the mid-1980s

Species	Great Saltee	Little Saltee	Total
Fulmar	325	142	467
Manx Shearwater	100+	< 50	c.150
Gannet	580-610	0	580-610
Cormorant	0	208	208
Shag	440-465	71	511-536
Great Black-backed Gull	70-100	250*	320-350*
Lesser Black-backed Gull	75-90	150*	225-240*
Herring Gull	< 2,600	2,000*	< 4,600*
Kittiwake	2,900	17	2,917
Razorbill	3,550-4,675	c.300	3,850-4,975
Guillemot	14,425-16,950	0	14,425-16,950
Puffin	1,100-1,200	< 30	1,130-1,230

* These three species have not been censused recently on Little Saltee. It is believed there have been decreases since the mid-1970s. The figures given here relate to the 1970s.

Bibliography

In the compilation of this book on the Saltees, it was found helpful to consult the following works. (Other references will be found in the footnotes).

Adams, C. L., *Castles of Ireland – Some Fortress Histories and Legends*, Elliott Stock, 1904.

Anderson, Ernest B., *Sailing Ships of Ireland*, Morris & Co., Dublin.

Andrews, J. H., *Ireland in Maps*, Dublin, 1961.

Barrington, Sir Jonah, *Personal Sketches of his own times* (1827-32).

Bassett, George Henry, *Wexford – County Guide and Directory*, Dublin, 1885.

Boate, *Natural History of Ireland*.

Burke, *Irish Family Records*, Burke's Peerage Ltd., London, 1976.

Burke, *Landed Gentry of Ireland*, 1958.

Cloney, Thomas, *A Personal Narrative of 1798*, 1832.

Dickson, Charles, *The Wexford Rising in 1798*, Kerryman, Tralee.

Doyle, Martin (Rev. William Hickey), *Notes and Gleanings relating to the County of Wexford*, Dublin, 1868.

Esmonde and Grogan Family MSS, National Library, Dublin.

Fraser, Robert, *Statistical Survey of the County of Wexford*, 1807.

Griffiths, George, *Chronicles of the County Wexford*, 1877.

Griffith, Sir Richard, *First Valuation of Ireland*, 1844; *General Valuation of Ireland*, 1853.

Hall, Mr. and Mrs. S. C., *Ireland – Its scenery, character, etc.*, Hall, Virtue and Co. London, 1855.

Hall, Mrs. S. C., *Sketches of Irish Character*, 1845.

Hayes, Richard, *Manuscript Sources for a History of Ireland*, National Library, Dublin.

Hore, Philip Herbert, *History of the Town and County of Wexford*, Elliott Stock, London, 1901.

Hore, P. H., *Barony Book – Bargy*, Hore MSS collection, St. Peter's College, Wexford.

Joyce, P. W., *The Origin and History of Irish Names of Places*, 1875.

Kinahan, G. H., *Explanatory Memoir of the Geological Survey of Ireland*, Alex. Thom and Hodges, Foster and Figgis, 1879.

Lewis, Samuel, *Topographical Dictionary of Ireland*, 1837.

Lynam, E., *The Mapmaker's Art*, London, 1953.

Macalister, R. A. S., *Corpus Inscriptionum*, National Library, Dublin.

Mason, Shaw, *Parochial Survey of Ireland*.

Mason, Thomas H., *The Islands of Ireland*, 1936, Revised edition, Mercier Press, 1967.

Mason, William Monck, *Hibernia Antiqua et Hodierna*, 1819.

Maxwell, W. H., *History of the Irish Rebellion in 1798*, H. G. Bohn, London, 1854.

McCall, P. J., *Selected Ballads and Poems*, '98 Commemoration Association, 1955.

McCormick, Donald, *Islands of Ireland*, Osprey Publishing Ltd., Berkshire, 1974.

McDowell, William, *The Shape of Ships*, Hutchinson, 1956.

Mitchell, Frank, *The Irish Landscape*, Collins, 1976.

O'Donovan, John, *Ordnance Survey Name Books*, Ordnance Survey, Phoenix Park, Dublin.

O'Riordain, Sean P., *Antiquities of the Irish Countryside*, University Paperbacks, Methuen, 1942.

Pakenham, Thomas, *The Year of Liberty*, Hodder and Stoughton, 1969.

Praeger, Robert Lloyd, *The Botanist in Ireland*, Hodges Figgis, 1934.

Praeger, R. L., *The Way That I Went*, Hodges, Figgis; Methuen, 1937.

Sailing Directions for the Coast of Ireland, Part I, British Admiralty, 1885.

Seward, Wm. Wenman, *Topographica Hibernica*, Dublin 1795.

Stokes, G. T., *Ireland and the Anglo-Norman Church*, Hodder and Stoughton, London, 1889.

The Land Problem in Ireland and its Settlement, Kevin R. O'Sheil and T. O'Brien, Irish Land Commission, Dublin.

Whittow, J. B., *Geology and Scenery in Ireland*, Penguin, 1974.

Worsaae, J. J. A., *An Account of the Danes and Norwegians in England, Scotland and Ireland*, John Murray, London, 1852.

ORNITHOLOGICAL BIBLIOGRAPHY

Only a few publications concern themselves wholly or mainly with the birds of the Saltee Islands, but a number of works contain useful references and the main ones are given here:

Cramp, S. Bourne, W. R. P., Saunders, D. *The Seabirds of Britain and Ireland*. Collins. London. 1974.

Kennedy, P. G., Ruttledge, R. F., Scroope, C. F. *The Birds of Ireland*. Oliver & Boyd. Edinburgh. 1954.

Mason, T. H. *The Islands of Ireland*. Mercier Press. Cork. 1967 (reprint).

Merne, O. J. *The Birds of Wexford, Ireland*. Irish Tourist Board, Dublin. 1974.

Perry, K. W., Warburton, S. W. *The Birds and Flowers of the Saltee Islands*. Perry & Warburton. Belfast. 1976.

Ruttledge, R. F. (Ed.). *Irish Bird Report*. Irish Ornithologists' Club. Dublin. 1953-1963.

Ruttledge, R. F. *Migrant and other birds of Great Saltee, Co. Wexford*. Proc. Royal Ir. Academy, 63 B 4. Dublin. 1963.

Ruttledge, R. F. *Ireland's Birds*. Witherby. London. 1966.

Ruttledge, R. F. *A List of the Birds of Ireland*. National Museum of Ireland. Dublin. 1975.

Sharrock, J. T. R. *An Atlas of Breeding Birds of Britain and Ireland*. Poyser. Berkhamstead. 1975.

Ussher, R. J., Warren, R. *The Birds of Ireland*. Gurney & Jackson. London. 1900.

Acknowledgments

Many people have helped in the compilation of this book. To the following in particular I wish to express my appreciation and thanks, whether it be for information and advice, the loan of books, manuscripts, maps, photographs, cuttings and other material, or just plain criticism.

Jack Devereux, Kilmore Quay, whose vast store of local knowledge was always at my disposal; John Sutton, Honorary Secretary, Kilmore Quay Life-Boat station; John Weaving, c/o Emerald Star Line, somewhere on the Shannon; Mrs. Liz Jefferies, Ballask, Kilmore; Eamonn Doyle, Kilmore Quay; Philip B. Pierce, Foxrock, Dublin; Mrs. Helen Skrine, Butlerstown Castle; Danny and Rosaleen Hassett, Rathronan Castle; Col. C. J. Davison, Bargy Castle, Mrs. Bettina Grattan Bellew, Mount Loftus, Goresbridge; John Grace, Enniscorthy; Micheal S. Meirtneach, Dublin; John Scanlon, Wexford; Nicholas Furlong, Drinagh; Jack Cahill and Kevin Stafford, Kilmore; John Barry, Kilmore Quay; the late Billy Kelly, Strand Hotel, Rosslare; Tom Walsh, Duncannon; Dr. John de Courcy Ireland, Dalkey; Stephen O'Sullivan, Dun Laoire; J. L. Boxwell, Dalkey; John Maddock, Cullenstown; Mrs. R. Egan, Scar; Tom Williams, Taghmon; "Bargyman"; Mrs. Katherine Ryan, Skerries; Seamus Geraghty, Dublin; Harry Neville, Ballymitty; Dr. Ned Culleton, An Foras Taluntais; Dr. Michael Max, Geological Survey of Ireland; Pat Crane, Enniscorthy; V. L. Mullowney, Dublin; Kit Fox, Skerries; Dr. Austin O'Sullivan, Johnstown Castle Research Centre; Patrick Crane and Pat Keenan, Dublin; Brendan Hearne, Dublin; Frank Healy and Paddy Farrell, "Irish Independent" Dublin; Comdt. Ray Roche, Athlone; Willy Bates, Kilmore Quay; Jim Maddock, Rosslare Harbour; Larry Bird, Fethard. My sincere thanks also to the following institutions and individual members of their staffs for assistance:

Commissioners of Irish Lights, Dublin, and Michael Costeloe; Ordnance Survey Office, Phoenix Park, and Sgt. Peter Fields; Placenames Office, Ordnance Survey and Dr. Alan Mac an Bhaird; the Director of the National Museum, Dr. Joseph Raftery and Padraig O Snodaigh and Michael Ryan; Registry of Deeds, King's Inns, and staff; Land Registry Office, Dublin; Valuation Office, Dublin; Secretary, Wexford County Council, and Miss B. Doyle; T. M. Dinan, Librarian, Lloyd's, London; Royal National Life-Boat Institution, Dublin, and Philip F. Mahony; Southeast Tourism and Miss Catherine Devitt; Public Record Office, Dublin, and staff; Public Record Office, London, and Alice Prochaska, National Army Museum, London, and P. B. Boyden, Dept. of Books and Archives; Maritiem Museum "Prins Hendrik", Rotterdam; Nederlandsch Historisch Maritiem Museum, Amsterdam; National Library, Dublin, director and staff; County Museum, Enniscorthy, Rev. T. Scallan and Committee; Hydrographic Dept., British Ministry of Defence, and A. T. Reynolds, Wreck Section; Folklore Commission, Belfield, Dublin, director and staff.

I also acknowledge, with thanks, permission from Messrs. Collins, London, to quote from Frank Mitchell's *The Irish Landscape*; permission to reproduce letters from the 1798 Collection in the State Papers Office, Dublin Castle, courtesy of the Keeper of State Papers; permission to reproduce various maps, courtesy of the Director, Ordnance Survey, Phoenix Park, Dublin; permission to use aerial photograph of the Great Saltee, from the "Irish Independent", Dublin.

RICHARD ROCHE

I would like to thank Major R. F. Ruttledge for first introducing me to the Saltee Islands over sixteen years ago when I visited the Bird Observatory on Great Saltee; Prince Michael I of the Saltees for permission to stay on Great Saltee on many subsequent occasions; Willie Bates and Jack Devereux for their helpfulness and skill in landing me, my family and colleagues, on Great Saltee, and taking us off again, sometimes in difficult conditions; the many ornithologists, too numerous to mention, who have diligently recorded their observations on the bird life of the islands, thereby making my task of writing about the birds very much easier than if I had to rely solely on my own observations — in this respect I would particularly like to acknowledge the usefulness of the published works of Major Ruttledge and Kenneth Perry on the birds of the Saltees.

OSCAR MERNE

ILLUSTRATIONS: We would like to thank and acknowledge the following for permission to reproduces photographs and illustrations: George Gmelch pages 1, 2, 7, 11, 14, 22, 94, 104, 105, 115, 127, 147, 148. Kelly's Hotel Rosslare (from a film of the Saltees) 14; Brendan Hearne 6 right and centre, 17, 37, 40, 55, 81 right, 84, 91; Richard Mills 6, 16, 20, 62, 81 left, 101, 104, 105, 110, 119, 123, 129, 132, 134, 138, 141, 143. H.M. Stationery Office and the Hydrographer of the Navy (portion of BA Chart No.2740) 72; Irish Independent 24 (bottom), 25 (top), Richard Roche 51; Maritiem Museum Rotterdam 29; Maxwell's *History of the Irish Rebellion 1798* engraved by George Cruickshank, 55 top; Oscar Merne 127; National Library of Ireland 19, 32, 34, 50; National Museum of Ireland 22, 25 (bottom), 32; Patrick Keenan (drawing) 22; Philip B. Pierce 84 (top); State Papers Office Dublin 57.

151